Weightless

Receiving Freedom from Lies About Your Weight & Value.

© Copyright 2023 JILL BLUE

All rights reserved. This book is protected by the copyright laws of the United States of America. This book may not be copied or reprinted for commercial gain or profit. The use of short quotations or occasional page copying for personal or group study is permitted and encouraged.

Scripture quotations taken from the Amplified® Bible (AMP), Copyright © 2015 by The Lockman Foundation. Used by permission. lockman.org

Scripture quotations marked (ESV) are from ESV® Bible (The Holy Bible, English Standard Version®), copyright © 2001 by Crossway, a publishing ministry of Good News Publishers. Used by permission. All rights reserved. All emphasis within Scripture quotations is the author's own.

Scripture quotations marked MSG are taken from The Message, copyright © 1993, 2002, 2018 by Eugene H. Peterson. Used by permission of NavPress. All rights reserved. Represented by Tyndale House Publishers.

"Scripture quotations taken from the (NASB®) New American Standard Bible®, Copyright © 1960, 1971, 1977, 1995, 2020 by The Lockman Foundation. Used by permission. All rights reserved. lockman.org."

Scripture quotations taken from The Holy Bible, New International Version® NIV® Copyright © 1973, 1978, 1984, 2011 by Biblica, Inc. Used with permission. All rights reserved worldwide.

Scripture taken from the New King James Version®. Copyright © 1982 by Thomas Nelson. Used by permission. All rights reserved.

Scripture quotations marked TPT are from The Passion Translation®. Copyright © 2017, 2018, 2020 by Passion & Fire Ministries, Inc. Used by permission. All rights reserved. ThePassionTranslation.com.

Acknowledgments

First of all, I want to thank you God- my Father, sweet Jesus, precious Holy Spirit- for the incredible healing and restoration you have brought me through your love and redemption. Without you, there would be no me, and there would be no book. I give you all honor, glory, and praise for ALL the great things you have done. I pray you are exalted in this book and that the name of Jesus is lifted high because of it.

To Desmond, my hue, thank you for championing me. Thank you for seeing my gifts and calling them out before I ever believed. Your love and choice to honor and serve me in the toughest times has healed my heart in ways that the Father knew, and I thank Him for sending you. It is a joy and privilege to be your wife. I love you forever. HOH-HO

To my Mama, you have been my cheerleader and BFF for so many years! Thank you! Thank you for allowing the Lord to heal and restore you and for ending cycles of generational curses through your obedience and surrender to the power of the cross! It's my honor to be your daughter. I rise up and call you blessed!

To AK for helping with the design, cover, and Canva :) for listening to the process for hours and for all the prayers. Thank you. I love you, friend.

To my dear friends who have trudged through the valley of healing with me, for those who encouraged, warred in prayer, cast out demons, called me higher, loved me in my weakness, and poured out truth, I thank you with all my heart and love you all.

To my Weightless Book Launch Team, thank you for your prayers, support, and encouragement. Your support has been invaluable! I appreciate and honor each of you.

To you, dear reader, thank you for coming along and joining the journey. I am praying for you as you travel. All my love. -Jill

Contents

Foreword	i
Introduction	iii
My Story	vi
Lie #1. "Skinniness is Next to Godliness"	1
Lie #2. "It's All My Fault"	15
Lie #3. "I'd Be Valuable If…"	31
Lie #4. "I'm Not Worth the Effort…"	45
Lie #5. "Love is All You Need."	57
Lie #6. "I'm Not Enough."	75
Lie #7. "God is Not Enough."	87
Lie #8. "I'll Never Be Free."	101
Lie #9. "I Can't Forgive Them."	113
Epilogue	121
Lie Breakers	123
Notes & Reference	134
Scripture Index	139

Foreword

If you're holding this book I am so excited for the freedom ahead for you!! How do I know freedom is on it's way? Almost 10 years ago, not fully believing I needed it, my daughter took my hand and pulled me through a door that was the beginning of a new life- full of freedom. Jill held a secret that she has walked so many people through. This secret was hard won.

I look back at every year of her life. I can remember her very first moments, her toddler defiance, her quiet submission, walking gently through her dad fighting for his life and bursting into HER life in collage, spreading her wings then her encounter with the Trinity and surrendering into the arms of God, allowing him to gently lead her into truth that has been described here beautifully. Truth you are meant for! This, like the day I held Jill for the first time is a Red Letter Day for you sweet one.

Lord, call this reader into all the more you have for them. Close their ears to the enemy and draw them into your precious freedom and help them to turn and give away wholeness and freedom to those around them.

Patrice McLuhan
(Jill's Mom and Realtor Extraordinaire)

Introduction

Writing this book was never in my plans. Although I have always been passionate about words, I never intended to share them on sensitive topics such as weight, diet, culture, exercise, and body image. These topics are often filled with opinions, hurts, and fears. However, in 2019, the Lord began leading me through a place of intimate connection with Him that led me into deep healing wells. He showed me that He "leaves no stone unturned." I heard Him whisper, "Write the book." I was unsure (or maybe too scared to pinpoint) what He was referring to. Over several months, through prayer, reading the Word, and conversations with friends, I realized the lies surrounding weight and value were the topics He wanted me to write about. So, in August of 2020, I started to write this book.

I told God, "Ok, I will do this. But, Holy Spirit, YOU have to do this." In other words, my flesh was willing to pen the words, but my spirit knew it MUST receive input from Holy Spirit. It took me years to get through the writing process. Sometimes, I sat down to write and couldn't see the screen for my tears because a little more healing came with every word I typed. I'll be honest: **I needed this book.**

Being transparent with the pain I've experienced and the lies I've believed has emptied me of the things I once felt consumed by. It has revealed areas in my life that needed additional healing, and the Lord has been faithful in filling me with His truth and love. He is so kind and generous in his love for us. And SOO, very patient. Throughout the process, I had an alarm on my phone going off twice a day, saying, **'Write the book.'** It still took YEARS to finish. Obedience to the Lord sometimes looks like one sentence at a time because processing and learning are part of the journey.

As I have written, I have prayed for you. You are the reason this book was written. I could have never penned these words, but Holy Spirit reminded me that all He has revealed and healed in me is not my own and that I must give it away. You are the one He had in mind when He told me to write. You are the one that He is calling into His marvelous light. You are the one that He desires to fill, heal, and restore. You are His chosen treasure, the one He adores, and He desires that you live in TOTAL freedom, body, soul, and spirit. I pray that these words fall on good ground and that they take root and flourish within you.

Papa,

Thank you for the one reading this book. Thank you for crafting them in your image, whole and complete, lacking nothing. I pray that even now, you are preparing their spirit to receive new and fresh revelation of how much you love them and how greatly you desire that they live free of all bondage. Please send angels around them now to guard against every lie that would try to speak to them as they read. I ask that they would only hear your voice that is constantly speaking truth over them "**...And I pray that you, being rooted and established in love, may have power, together with all the Lord's holy people, to grasp how wide and long and high and deep is the love of Christ, and to know this love that surpasses knowledge—that you may be filled to the measure of all the fullness of God." Ephesians 3:17-19 NIV**
Amen.

My story

I have always been aware of body image and weight. From the time I was a little girl, I remember hearing my parents, grandparents, aunts, and cousins discussing body images. Whether they were downplaying themselves or someone else (In a "bless their heart" manner), I learned that people held intense opinions about weight and body image.

As a child, I began to gain weight quickly, and I can remember my parents attempting to monitor my food intake to assist me in losing weight. I picked up on the fact that my food experience differed from my brothers. They were active and thin and did not carry excess weight. I know my parents had no harmful intent behind their actions, but they shared the belief that people view overweight girls differently than thin ones. I'm sure they were also concerned about my health, but the message I internalized from some of their words and actions was, "Fat is ugly. No guy will like you if you are fat."

I remember feeling the need to hide my food or to eat quickly before someone discovered me eating something like candy or ice cream. I felt a lot of shame surrounding my eating habits. I continued growing and was a tall child, but with that, I was bigger than most of the other girls. I was never the smallest or thinnest in my classes.

Growing up, I watched my mom struggle with a lot of insecurities surrounding her body and eating. After four pregnancies before she was 27 years old, her body changed, and she was not altogether comfortable with what she saw in the mirror. She and my dad met when she was 14, and she no longer held the figure of a young girl but a woman. My dad preferred a thin woman, and I think she internalized his preferences and equated her value to her size. Her struggles with body image were sometimes shared, as she is a verbal processor (like me), and I began to think that speaking negatively about my body was normal.

Jill in 1998

In middle school, my classmates bullied me about my curly, frizzy hair, glasses, and size. As one of the tallest kids in my class, I never felt like I fit in. By the age of 11, I began to feel the threads of depression wrapping themselves around me. Looking back at the journals I kept from that time, I realize that even at 11 years old, I was having thoughts of self-harm and fantasizing about "not being around anymore."

Jill in 1998

My high school years began, and my thoughts of self-hatred were at an all-time high. My father was diagnosed with cancer, and everything in my life turned upside down. It seemed like chaos was all around, and everything was out of control.

I didn't realize it then, but my desire to control something in my life led to control over my food and looks. This desire for control led to restricted eating and attempts at bulimia. I still thank God today for the friends who saw my actions and told my school counselor, who walked me away from that behavior.

After my father died in 2002, I began to experience panic attacks and worsening depression. I straightened my hair every day to erase the memory of those frizzy curls.

Jill in 2003

By 2003, as a freshman in college, negative thoughts about myself were consuming. I was constantly comparing myself to others, and in my eyes, I always came up wanting.

I ate only salads and cottage cheese most of my Freshman year because I had heard of the dreaded "Freshman 15," and I refused to gain weight. I went through times of intensely exercising to beat my body into looking a certain way. Everything I did revolved around being skinny. I wanted to be attractive to guys and esteemed by other women. To have all of your thoughts bound to those motives is exhausting. I would walk into rooms and feel the weight of every eye on my form and feel disgusted by what they must think of me. In reality, people probably did not even notice me entering. Thoughts of those days bring me to tears in part because of the physical pain they produced in me and in part because of how crippled I was in my effectiveness in life.

When we are self-consumed by depressive and oppressive thought patterns, we are unable to see and effectively meet the needs of those around us.

During my college years, I had a lot of doubts and insecurities while dating. I often felt like I wasn't good enough - not skinny, not unique, not funny enough - just never enough. However, when I started dating my husband Desmond in 2008, he showed me a different kind of love - one that came without conditions. One evening, we were hanging out watching TV and decided to go to the store to get some dinner. I was in my sweats and told him I needed to change. He grabbed my hand and asked why I was going to change. Surprised, I said, "I need to look cute to go out." Desmond stopped me and hugged me, saying, "You never have to change to be with me. You're always cute, and it doesn't matter what you wear - sweats or dressed up, it doesn't change you."

At that moment, I finally felt loved for who I was for the first time. But to be honest, getting what you've always wanted without healing from past pain can make it hard to trust and accept the love you've always desired.

Desmond and I got engaged on November 7, 2009. I entered our marriage on August 21, 2010, believing my husband's love would help me overcome my emotional wounds and insecurities. However, this unrealistic thinking brought high expectations for my husband, which he was neither equipped nor obligated to fulfill. Through all of my insecurities and doubts, Father was working. He was shaping my heart to His. In the moments I felt like my failures were the mountain I couldn't move

He was looking at me from the other side, seeing me as whole, restored, complete, and lacking nothing. He knew the journey would not be easy, but he had equipped me before the foundations of the earth for the good works he had prepared for me. As my mom says "He packed my bag" for this road.

Desmond & Jill in 2016

In 2016, I was at my heaviest weight and the most unhealthy place in my life. I was struggling with hypertension, high blood sugar, and Polycystic Ovary Syndrome (PCOS). I led a sedentary and depressed lifestyle, which in turn led to more depression, anxiety, and health issues. My husband and I had not been preventing pregnancy since 2011. After a chemical pregnancy in 2012 and no children since, I was feeling defeated and barren.

This was a dark time in my life. I slipped into disordered eating. An addiction to sugar and high-carbohydrate foods consumed me. I craved them. It became so unhealthy that I was sneaking candy in the middle of the night, and eating dessert after breakfast. It was severe, and I didn't know how to stop.

I was constantly exhausted, requiring 1-2 naps a day, partially because of the intense sugar highs and crashes and partially because of the depression. I felt utterly defeated. I had walked with God since I was a child, but I was not walking closely with him. I did not spend time with him or his word; all I heard were lies in my head. I had no idea how to break out of the cycle I found myself in. Suicidal thoughts crept in often. In the Summer of 2016, a friend told me about a new way of eating called the Ketogenic Diet (To clarify, this is my story, and I am not stating that this way of eating is for everyone.)

I began to study this way of eating to discern if it was an option that would benefit my body. It felt overwhelming, and I wasn't interested. It took me several months to conclude that I needed to switch. And even then, it took longer before I decided to start. I had lived a "diet-culture" life for so long that this felt like one more thing I would fail.

There was a day in October 2016 when I felt the gentle pressing of the Lord to let go of the control (or lack thereof) of my eating. I don't know about you, but that feeling often leads to a sense of panic because I start to think that I need to know the next steps and how to move when I have no idea. This is often paralyzing. But this time, I yelled at God, **"I cannot do another diet, I cannot do this ANY MORE! YOU HAVE TO DO THIS!"** It was that moment of surrender that sounded like anger and desperation that led me into my current life of freedom I did not know was possible. After just two months of following a strict keto protocol, my periods began to regulate. At my next physical a few months later, my blood work showed that I was no longer in an unhealthy blood sugar range. I began losing weight and dress sizes and felt confidence blooming. I started walking and then began doing workouts from home. I continued on a strict keto diet for about two years and, in that time, dropped two more dress sizes. I began to increase my workouts, and I maintained my weight loss. I became less strict in my diet around 2019 but remained low-carb, and today, I still stay completely off of sugar and wheat and exercise 2-3 times a week.

In December 2019, I began to feel a shift in my spirit; it was as if the Lord was letting me in on the fact that change was coming. He began to show me that his love and mercy are unchangeable and that it is impossible for him to lie to me. Earlier in the year I was asked to lead a young women's retreat and in March 2020, just two weeks before everything shut down I led the retreat with the theme **Steadfast**.

The Lord led me to **Hebrews 6:18-19** which says, **"so that by two unchangeable things [His promise and His oath] in which God can't lie, we who have fled [to Him] for refuge would have strong encouragement and indwelling strength to hold tightly to the hope set before us. This hope [this confident assurance] we have as an anchor of the soul [it cannot slip and it cannot break down under whatever pressure bears upon it]—a safe and steadfast hope that enters within the veil."** That weekend set into motion a new understanding that Christ is my firm foundation, my cornerstone. He is the anchor in a sea of storms and the love that holds me through it all.

As of August 2023, I have lost four dress sizes and a total loss of over 50 pounds- although I did gain 20 and then lose that again, which makes the weight loss more like 70 pounds. I no longer struggle with symptoms of high blood sugar, PCOS, or high cholesterol. I don't require a nap to get through the day, and I feel healthier and stronger than ever. However, all those benefits pale in comparison to the true healing that took place and is still ongoing in my spirit. Fall of 2020, I experienced a supernatural deliverance through the power of the Holy Spirit, where I was delivered from the weight of grief, an actual oppression by the spirit of heaviness that had crippled me since the death of my father.

A few months later, in January 2021, another supernatural healing occurred when I was delivered and set free from the oppressive spirit of rejection. I had carried around the lie that people were judging me, that I was ugly and not enough my whole life, and when Jesus freed me of that lie, true freedom and healing took place.

When I see people I have not seen in a few years, they often do not recognize me. This is primarily due to the extreme change in my spiritual countenance. The sweetness of Jesus and his love changes EVERYTHING. When we submit to him and allow Him space, He heals, frees, and restores all that is stolen. **Joel 2:25** states, **"And I will compensate you for the years that the swarming locust has eaten, the creeping locust, the stripping locust, and the gnawing locust..."** God will return even the parts of your life wasted in unhealthy, un-godly pursuits. His love for you is limitless, and it is waiting for you to grab ahold of it.

"Praise God, everybody!
Applaud God, all people!
His love has taken over our lives;
God's faithful ways are eternal.
Hallelujah!"
Psalm 117 The Message

Section 1: The Lies

Lie #1
"Skinniness is next to Godliness."

Social perceptions of weight and beauty

Have you ever noticed how hairstyles come in trends? For example, when I was in middle school and the TV show, 'Friends' was at its peak, all my friends started styling their hair like Jennifer Aniston's character, Rachel. Her straight hair with many layers and iconic middle part became a staple among American women and girls. With my thick, curly hair, I could not acquire this popular style because we did not have flat irons or creams then. I'll never forget my mom taking a towel and our household IRON to my curls to persuade them into straightness. I wanted to look like everyone else, even though I was born to be uniquely me. Similarly, the "ideal figure" that still haunts women and girls began shortly after supermodel 'Twiggy' became famous in the 1960s. Her long, thin frame quickly became the standard of the fashion world.

I'm sure you've seen the effects as you flipped through magazines filled with waif-like models and watched movies starring super-thin "perfect" actresses. **Idealism has a way of choking out uniqueness.** I've heard plus-sized women describe how men don't hold doors open for them, of how people stare at them while they eat. The stories of the terrible ways parents, teachers, bosses, boyfriends, and especially peers have treated them have brought me to tears.

I've experienced some of these injustices in my own life. When I was 16, I went to a water park with friends. I stood in line for a ride in my tankini with my friends and classmates. A guy I barely knew looked down at my hips and made fun of the "rivers" I had there. He was referring to the thin, white stretch marks that told the story of my quick rise to my now 5 feet 7 inches. I was one of the tallest students in my fifth-grade class. I suffered from terrible 'growing pains'. I received the aforementioned stretch marks on my hips as I grew to the height I now appreciate. But, that day, at such a vulnerable age, I remember feeling the bile rise in my throat and an internal trembling start as he spoke those words.

Even now, as I write that story, I can remember the location the pain went into my body. My physical body received a lot of damage due to the words and trauma I experienced, especially as a child and teenager. The Lord has graciously taken me on a healing journey that has freed my physical body from pain and grief. It has not been an easy or short process, and I pray that you will not grow weary in your healing journey, especially if it has taken longer than you would like.

Words have power.

It's no wonder that these powerful words that others speak over us, which we then repeat out loud or in our minds, lead to severe repercussions. One of those repercussions is disordered eating. Disordered eating can show up in different ways, such as anorexia nervosa, bulimia nervosa, and binge-eating disorder. Compulsive exercise and other restrictive behaviors surrounding food and weight are also prevalent in those who suffer from body dysmorphia- a type of compulsive disorder that causes the individual to suffer from a distorted view of self. An astounding 30 million Americans live with some form of eating disorder. 15% of women have had eating disorder symptoms, and 28% of adults in America will suffer from eating disorders at some point in their lives. Sadly, someone dies approximately every 52 minutes due to the results of an eating disorder.

My Journey

In the fall of 1999, I entered public high school after years of homeschooling and Christian school. As a Freshman, I was inundated with a whole new world of expectations of beauty and felt the pressures to conform to them like never before. In the second semester of that year, my father was diagnosed with cancer, and my life turned upside down. I was 14, terrified, insecure, and grasping for something to hold onto. So, in an attempt to lose weight and, more than anything, to feel control over something, I started restricting my food and made attempts- thankfully feeble ones- at purging. My restrictions and strange behaviors in the restroom

---

National Association of Anorexia Nervosa and Associated Disorders (n.d.). General Eating Disorder Statistics. ANAD.com. Retrieved November 15, 2023, from https://anad.org/eating-disorder-statistic/#general

prompted my friends to speak to my school counselor, who called me to his office and scared the bulimia away. I am forever grateful to those friends who not only recognized the signs of disordered eating but made moves to help me. I have often wondered where I might have been without their intervention.

Jill on the left in 1999

The wild thing is that I had always known about the dangers of anorexia and bulimia because I grew up hearing about the death of one of my grandfather's favorite singers, Karen Carpenter, who died due to heart failure after years of anorexia. But, even armed with knowledge about the dangers, I fell into the lie that I was not enough, that I needed to "fit in," and that at my weight, I didn't.

I remember looking in the mirror as a young woman and genuinely feeling disgusted at what I saw. There have been very few times I've ever felt that way about another person, yet I felt them about myself every day for years. What we think, we say & what we say, we become. I thought that because I didn't look like the skinny girls at church and school, I was disgusting. A failure. A disappointment... This thought pattern led to insecurities that formed into mountains that blocked me from developing friendships and experiencing life to the fullest.

I attended a Disciple Now weekend retreat in middle school with my youth group. These weekends taught students about Jesus and how to be His disciples. They were a time to bond, have fun, and learn about others in your youth groups. This weekend was held at the home of a family in our church. Their daughter, a year older than me, was beautiful. Naturally tall, thin, blonde, and so sweet! She was a favorite among the youth, and she intimidated me. The thing I remember most about that weekend was how depressed and angry I was and how out of place I felt. At one point, I remember all the girls were upstairs in a big loft room, watching movies, braiding hair, laughing, and talking, and I felt shunned. No one had said or done anything negative, but because no one had told me something positive about myself or intentionally called for me to join in, I felt rejected. The lies in my head were so loud. I remember leaving the room and hiding in the spare bedroom, with the desperate hope that someone would come looking for me. I wanted to see that they wanted me to be there. After a while, someone came looking for me. She tried to comfort me and tell me I was accepted, but her words didn't fit or fill the hole inside me. We often feel that if the right person says the right things, our hearts will be mended, and we will no longer feel the heart-breaking rejection. This is a lie. GOD is the ONLY one who can heal the rejection, the hurt, the fill-in-the-blank.

"...He has also planted eternity [a sense of divine purpose] in the human heart [a mysterious longing which nothing under the sun can satisfy, except God]..."
Ecclesiastes 3:11 AMP

Each of us has a hole created by God to be filled by Him. He desires for us to desire Him. Much like ladies often desire the men in our lives to WANT to WANT to do things, He wants us to want Him. He does not force our hearts into relationship, but He created in us the ability to KNOW that we NEED it. The problem lies in the need for clarification of that need. When we start running on feelings, we miss the entire point. We live a life that is focused on "Fulfilling our needs" when, in fact, we are still empty inside. We date around, looking for "the one" who will make us feel beautiful. We work, work, work to prove that we are "good enough." We place things, people, money, sex, addictions... the list could go on and on into that hole, trying so hard to feel complete. And all the while, we feel depleted. Running on fumes. Running on self.

"Are you tired? Worn out? Burned out on religion? Come to me. Get away with me, and you'll recover your life. I'll show you how to take a real rest. Walk with me and work with me—watch how I do it. Learn the unforced rhythms of grace. I won't lay anything heavy or ill-fitting on you. Keep company with me and you'll learn to live freely and lightly."
Matthew 11: 28-30 The Message

Strongholds

A stronghold is a defense system. In ancient times, people built massive walls as a defense system to guard them against ruthless attacks. They fashioned tall, thick walls and high towers where men could battle against invaders. These fortresses were often impregnable. However, an enemy could breach the walls. So, the fortresses often had a second line of defense at the city's heart, a stronghold. In this Stronghold, the people could ward off the enemy again. Satan has no power outside of his ability to deceive. **1 Peter 5:8** teaches, **"Be sober [well balanced and self-disciplined], be alert and cautious at all times. That enemy of yours, the devil, prowls around like a roaring lion [fiercely hungry], seeking someone to devour." AMP** We are to expect Satan to attack and are called to be prepared and resist him. **James 4:7** promises, **"So submit to [the authority of] God. Resist the devil [stand firm against him], and he will flee from you." AMP** Satan desires his thought patterns to infiltrate the minds of believers, which become strongholds in our minds.

We, as believers, are often victims of strongholds built up within us by our own words. The enemy will build a stronghold in us when we permit him. Satan is a legalist who requires your permission to infiltrate your mind. **We give the enemy permission by giving voice to subtle thoughts that often line up with our experiences but not God's word.** When we agree with Satan's lies and speak them over ourselves, the foundation of a stronghold forms.

For many years. I lived under the weight of a stronghold of rejection through the many cruel words I spoke over myself because of self-hatred and unforgiveness towards myself.

Strongholds begin with just one incident that produces a small **thought** created from a **fact-based lie**, a lie created based on a real-life situation, or a word spoken over you. If not uprooted, this lie will live in your head rent-free for years! You or others can also reinforce it, speaking it over you again and again. Therefore, the time of belief continues, and it feels natural to think like you do, even if it is all based on a lie- it's been years, right?

This lie will create thought patterns, where you may once again encounter a trauma or situation that affirms the lie and causes your thoughts to continually build the lie up and increase its weight in your life. This lie is now a Stronghold in your life, a tower of pain that has caused you to experience life through the lens of hurt, trauma, and lies instead of victory, forgiveness, and freedom.

Formulation of a Stronghold

Thought

Fact-based lie

Time of belief

Thought pattern

Stronghold

In middle school, I had a crush on a boy. Somehow, he found out I had a crush on him, and he made a nasty statement about me, basically saying that unless I suddenly started to look like a certain supermodel, he would never find me attractive. This statement created a thought about my looks. With my curly, frizzy brown hair, I looked NOTHING like the tall, skinny, blonde supermodel he was referring to, so therefore, the thought that I was ugly set in.

The fact was that I didn't look like the supermodel, but the belief that I was ugly because I looked different was a fact-based lie. That lie set in and began to take root. I was 11 years old when that incident occurred, and it was not uprooted from my life until I was 35, so the time of belief in the lie caused it to feel more accurate. There had been so many years of believing I was ugly that it felt natural and true.

Over the years, other boys made me feel ugly with their behavior and words, which created a thought pattern of constant self-abuse. Every time I walked into a room, I could feel every eye on me, and my thoughts would whisper, **"They all think you are so fat," "Everyone can see your double chin," "If you had just dieted more before this event you wouldn't look like you were squeezed into this dress," "you are disgusting."** The list could go on and on, and therein lies the Stronghold. I saw everything through this lie because the belief was foundational. I didn't know who I was without the running tab of disapproval that ran through my mind. It became my identity, and I regularly voiced those negatives about myself aloud for all to hear.

Every relationship I had suffered under the weight of this Stronghold, even my relationship with God. Having such terrible thoughts about myself led to a feeling that even God must have negative thoughts about me. I also could not understand why God "Made me fat" and "loved the skinny girls more than me." I placed such significant value on weight that I believed that God himself valued me differently than other girls based on their jean size. **John 10:10 AMP says, "The thief comes only in order to steal and kill and destroy..."** The thief, satan, builds a plan to corrupt and steal from our lives. He works against us in every way to steal the truth of our identity as daughters of the most high God. Many people say things like, 'Don't give satan so much credit.' While I agree that not everything is demonic, the reality is that a spiritual battle rages on around us whether we acknowledge it or not.

> **"For our struggle is not against flesh and blood, but against the rulers, against the authorities, against the powers of this dark world and against the spiritual forces of evil in the heavenly realms."**
> **Eph 6:12 AMP**

This verse shows us just how real the war around us really is. The fantastic thing is that we are not left defenseless. Jesus' death on the cross purchased for us the freedom and authority to walk as DAUGHTERS and SONS of the most high God. His death and resurrection equal our ability to combat every demonic thing that would attempt to raise weapons against us. **"Finally, be strong in the Lord and in his mighty power. Put on the full armor of God, so that you can take your stand against the devil's schemes." Eph 6:10-11 AMP**

This verse reveals to us that the Lord has prepared us for every battle because the complete victory is in Him. What does that look like in my everyday life? Like taking EVERY thought captive to the obedience of Christ. In other words, and in a unique translation from The Message, **"We use our powerful God-tools for smashing warped philosophies, tearing down barriers erected against the truth of God, fitting every loose thought and emotion and impulse into the structure of life shaped by Christ. Our tools are ready at hand for clearing the ground of every obstruction and building lives of obedience into maturity." 2 Cor 10:5 The Message**

One of the ways that I continually walk in freedom is to pray every day for the armor of God to be placed on me, to be shielded from the works of the enemy, and to take every thought captive, forcing any lies I hear to obey the truth of what God says about me.

"Therefore take up the whole armor of God, that you may be able to withstand in the evil day, and having done all, to stand. Stand therefore, having girded your waist with truth, having put on the breastplate of righteousness, and having shod your feet with the preparation of the gospel of peace; above all, taking the shield of faith with which you will be able to quench all the fiery darts of the wicked one. And take the helmet of salvation, and the sword of the Spirit, which is the word of God"
Ephesians 6:13-17 AMP

Below is a list of some of the common lies I told myself for years. I would look in the mirror and hear these terrible things in my own voice. As I listened to these things, I then spoke them out loud. I was not always intending to harm myself; in fact, I thought I was protecting myself by saying things before people thought them. I was "owning the fact" (lie) that I was "Fat" or that my "hair is awful," or I looked "terrible in these jeans." But these statements were lies that created a stronghold in my life.

"I am so fat."
"I am a failure."
"I don't belong here."
"I'm not smart enough."
"I will never be pretty like them."
"If I don't do my makeup I will look disgusting."
"Every photo of me is ugly."
"I will never be enough."
"No one wants me here."
"I look hideous."
"I'm an idiot."

Whenever I agree with a lie in any way, I verbally confess repentance for partnering with the lie, and then I replace it with the truth. The best way to combat lies is to consume the Word of God, which will always point you to Jesus and your true identity in Him.

The Lie: Skinniness is Next to Godliness

The lies that skinniness and your image are as important, or sometimes more than Godliness, is a warped view that the enemy will use to torment you. I want you to grab a piece of paper and a pen. Would you start by praying this aloud: **"Dear Jesus, would you come and reveal to me the lies that I have been believing?"** Now, could you take a moment to let him speak to you? Consider the lies that you have been believing and write them down.

The Lie Breaker

Read this prayer aloud with **BOLDNESS**! Step into the truth God has for you! Pray it daily, if needed. Take every thought captive- literally, grab the negative thoughts Satan spews at you and throw them out. Fill your heart with truth and hope from the Word.

"Father, I repent for agreeing with and I walk away from the lies I have believed that do not line up with your truth. I repent and walk away from self-hatred. I repent and walk away from negative self-talk. I repent and walk away from (Fill in your own here) _____. I receive the forgiveness you bought for me on the cross. I choose to forgive myself for (whatever you still feel angry with yourself about) _____. I receive the truth that I am loved, I am righteous through Jesus, and that my worth is rooted in you. I ask that you would come and heal the wounds on my soul. Amen."

Lie #2
"It's All My Fault"

The shame game.

Walking in the lie that your weight or body size is "all your fault" is simply not true. Condemnation and shame, two things Christ ended with His death on the cross, form this way of thinking. **"Therefore there is now no condemnation [no guilty verdict, no punishment] for those who are in Christ Jesus [who believe in Him as personal Lord and Savior]." Romans 8:1 AMP**

Because of the nature of this fallen world (the world after sin entered it) that we live in, many things combat the healthy and whole body Christ died to provide for us. Things like lack of movement, poor nutrition, unhealthy sleep, lack of adequate sunlight, demanding schedules, & nutrient deficiencies all play a role in the way our bodies thrive or falter.

One of the things I have seen growing over the past few years is the idea of "self-love" and "body positivity." While these concepts are not faulty in the generic sense, they are often a bandage over a gaping wound. When we try to love and speak positively about our bodies only regarding how our body looks, we are missing the more significant point. **"Have you forgotten that your body is now the sacred temple of the Spirit of Holiness, who lives in you? You don't belong to yourself any longer, for the gift of God, the Holy Spirit, lives inside your sanctuary. You were God's expensive purchase, paid for with tears of blood, so by all means, then, use your body to bring glory to God!"** 1 Cor 6:19-20 TPT

When we hyper-focus on the way our bodies look, we're missing the point that God created our bodies to glorify himself and to bring his love to all we meet. Words like "body-shaming" regarding discussing body type, size, health, etc., are sometimes thrown around to dissuade uncomfortable conversations. The need to be politically correct is often stronger than the need to be vulnerable and honest.

Some of us struggle with obesity and the diseases associated with it, making our daily lives challenging. Every day, things affect our bodies, and attempt to harm them. It's honestly astounding to see the resilience of the human body. Women's bodies are incredible as they can give birth, nurse, and nurture other humans! Our hormones carry a lot of responsibility for the daily operations of our bodies. Those hormones, which control things like our thyroid, adrenal glands, sleep, weight, and much more, can quickly become affected by the many things in this world that can harm them. I am not a doctor or nutritionist, so please do not take my words as science to live by or specific actions to take for yourself, but be encouraged that many different things play a role in our health and the ability for our bodies to thrive.

I recommend seeing a functional specialist, typically an MD, who facilitates a holistic approach that looks for root causes of symptoms and uses multiple modalities for healing. I see a Christian functional M.D. who has prayed for me in his office instead of giving me medication. I recommend having a blood panel drawn once a year to be sure that all of your body's needs are met and all levels are in the normal range. If they are not, a functional specialist can assist you in understanding how diet, movement, supplements, and lifestyle can work harmoniously to help your body function how God intended it to.

The following is a short, non-medical advice synopsis of some of the body's crucial elements and unctions. In these sections, you will learn some of the body's important functions as well as many of the areas that can experience deficiency, which can lead to weight gain, depression, anxiety, etc...

Thyroid

The Thyroid gland is a small gland in the neck that secretes hormones that regulate the body's temperature and weight and assist in the heart, brain, and other organs. If your thyroid becomes underactive weight gain can be a factor. The cause of the weight gain in those with hypothyroidism can be multifaceted and may not simply be at. Often the extra weight is due to an added excess of water and salt that is retained in the body. Having your doctor run detailed and specific Thyroid tests may assist you in determining if you have a Thyroid imbalance of any kind. While most doctors test for TSH, T4, and T3 total, an endocrinologist or Integrative specialist may order more advanced tests such as TSH, Free T3, Free T4, Total T4, Reverse T3, Total T3, T3 Uptake, Thyroglobulin Ab, TPO Ab to determine in detail how well your thyroid is functioning. Several online labs will allow you to order these tests for yourself to assist you in better understanding your body.

Adrenals

The Adrenals are two small glands in the back, above the kidneys. They work to "produce hormones that help regulate your metabolism, immune system, blood pressure, response to stress and other essential functions." The adrenals produce Cortisol and Adrenaline, which regulate other aspects of the body, such as energy and weight. They are crucial to your ability to sleep well and function with normal energy. Some use the term "adrenal fatigue" to describe the condition that arises when the adrenals have been 'overworked' through excessive stress and other conditions, such as reliance on high levels of caffeine. This fatigue can cause a host of issues in the body, such as exhaustion, brain fog, body aches, lack of motivation, etc.

You can imagine that the drive to exercise may not be available if these symptoms are present. I personally suffered from dysfunctional cortisol levels for years and struggled to get through the day without a nap. One of the

https://www.hopkinsmedicine.org/health/conditions-and-diseases/adrenal-glands

best things I was prescribed during this time was to cut out caffeine and lay down on my back for about 30 minutes in the middle of every day. The idea here is that your body may be in constant "fight or flight" mode, and it does not know when to calm itself and stop producing excess cortisol, which can turn into excess fat. Laying down midday may help to restore the correct levels of cortisol in the body and tell the nervous system that everything is ok.

> "YOUR BODY MAY BE IN CONSTANT 'FIGHT OR FLIGHT' MODE, AND IT DOES NOT KNOW WHEN TO CALM ITSELF AND STOP PRODUCING EXCESS CORTISOL, WHICH CAN TURN INTO EXCESS FAT."

Nutrition

One fascinating area is how food can heal or harm our bodies. The American diet typically consists of many pre-packaged foods that contain pesticides, food dyes, preservatives, "Natural Flavors," Genetically Modified Organisms (GMOs), excess sugar, and corn syrup.
The foods you may have grown up eating have changed DRASTICALLY over the past 30+ years. The food industry has shifted from farm to table to chemicals to box. Companies often forsake what is in the consumer's best interest for what is in the company's best financial interest.

Pesticides

One of the most well-known pesticides, sprayed on many crops you probably consume, is glyphosate. "Organophosphates, which were promoted as a more ecological alternative to organochlorines (58), include a great variety of pesticides, the most common of which is glyphosate. This class also includes other known pesticides, such as malathion, parathion, and dimethoate; some are known for their endocrine-disrupting potential". When disrupted, the endocrine system can negatively target your hormones, which can affect weight. It can also cause inflammation, which can appear to be weight gain, and can exacerbate underlying health problems, furthering the current struggles in the body.

Food dyes

Food dyes in our foods in the U.S. can creep in in many more areas than you might think. "Even some fresh oranges are dipped in dye to brighten them and provide uniform color". It has been concluded through testing "that the nine artificial dyes approved in the United States likely are carcinogenic (cancer-causing), cause hypersensitivity reactions and behavioral problems, or are inadequately tested." While the U.S. still uses these food dyes, other countries have realized these chemicals are harmful and stopped using them. "Food manufacturers still use plant-based colorings in some countries. For example, in the United Kingdom Fanta orange soda is colored with pumpkin and carrot extracts while the U.S. version uses Red 40 and Yellow 6. McDonald's strawberry sundaes are colored only with strawberries in Britain, but Red 40 is used in the United States."

Nicolopoulou-Stamati, Polyxeni et al. "Chemical Pesticides and Human Health: The Urgent Need for a New Concept in Agriculture." *Frontiers in public health* vol. 4 148. 18 Jul. 2016, doi:10.3389/fpubh.2016.00148

Preservatives

While many foods require preservation to remain viable long term, the preservation process is often at a high price to the health of the consumer. "as per the study of The American Cancer Society one must avoid consumption of these chemically treated meat food items as they increase the cancer, vomiting, asthma, nausea." (Kilfoy, et al., 2011). Healthline states, "Maybe it's not how much you eat, but something that's added to what you eat that's making you gain weight." The article references a study on how the preservative propionate "may be an endocrine disruptor that increases the risk of both diabetes and obesity in humans."

Genetically Modified Organisms (GMO)

The phrase 'GMO' and the labels touting 'NON-GMO' have crept into our culture over the last few decades, but many of us are not sure what that even means. A label of NON-GMO is often a misnomer because the foods within are not Genetically Modified, to begin with, and they are utilizing this label as a tactic to sell to a consumer concerned about GMOs. So, what are Genetically Modified Organisms anyway? According to the Non-GMO Project, GMOs are "a plant, animal, microorganism or other organism whose genetic makeup has been modified in a laboratory using genetic engineering or transgenic technology. This creates combinations of plant, animal, bacterial and virus genes that do not occur in nature or through traditional crossbreeding methods." So what is the big deal? The metabolic research center

Deepanksha Sharma, Shania Javed, Arshilekha, Prachi Saxena, Priyanka Babbar, Divyanshu Shukla, Priyanshi Srivastava and Siddh Food Additives and Their Effects: A Mini Review", International Journal of Current Research, 10, (06), 69999 Available online at http://www.journalcra.com
Potera C. (2010). The artificial food dye blues. *Environmental health perspectives, 118*(10), A428. https://doi.org/10.1289/ehp.118-a428
https://www.science.org/doi/10.1126/scitranslmed.aav0120
https://www.healthline.com/health-news/food-additive-can-lead-to-obesity-diabetes
https://www.science.org/doi/10.1126/scitranslmed.aav0120
https://www.healthline.com/health-news/food-additive-can-lead-to-obesity-diabetes

posits, "Genetically modified foods are structurally identical to their natural counterparts, but they do not break down the same nor are they easy for the body to utilize once they enter the body." This lack of breakdown may increase health risks as the foods do not carry the same intrinsic benefits or nutrients as their original counterparts. Foods known to contain GMOs:
Alfalfa (Often fed to animals that you may ingest later), Canola, Corn (also feed for animals such as cows, chickens, etc), Papaya, Soy, Sugar Beet (may be used to create sugar), Yellow Summer Squash, Zucchini, Potato.

Mental Health

Humans are magnificent creations made in the image of God. God is one in three parts: the Trinity- Father, Son (Jesus), & Holy Spirit; Humans are one in three parts: Body, Soul (Mind, Will & Emotions) & Spirit (our eternal being). Just as we need to commune with the Father, Son & Holy Spirit, we must also care for each part of ourselves. To neglect the body is to neglect the whole. To neglect the Soul is to neglect the whole. To neglect the Spirit is to neglect the whole. Mental health is connected to all three parts of humanity and has long been a point of conversation and confusion among Christians. While spiritual reasons bring on cases of mental illness, for this chapter, I will discuss the physical ramifications.

As of 2019, an estimated 19 million people in the U.S. had suffered from at least one major depressive episode. Depression is one of the most significant issues affecting people today. I believe that not all depression is spiritual, and not all depression is physical. To say otherwise would

---
https://www.nongmoproject.org/gmo-facts/what-is-gmo/
https://www.emetabolic.com/locations/centers/wichita-falls/blog/eat-well/can_genetic_modification_to_crops_effect_weight_gain/htmhttps://www.nimh.nih.gov/health/statistics/major-depression

be very limiting to the holistic creation of the human body. As we know, nutrition plays a significant role in the success of our bodies, and the quality of foods we eat is more important than ever. Julia Ross, Author of The Mood Cure, explains how food impacts mental and physical health. In the book, she shares quizzes that help determine if you may have a deficiency in amino acids, which are the building blocks of the brain. These deficiencies can create imbalances in the brain, leading to everything from depression & anxiety to cravings & addictions. She also goes into great detail about the quality of foods we eat and why their quality is vital to our health. According to Julia "gluten has been implicated in mental illness since at least 1979". She explains her belief that gluten actually binds to certain receptors in our brains leading to an addictive experience with certain foods, and to a depressive state when they are removed. This is just one example of many explaining how significantly foods impact our bodies and mental health.

Movement

How is your relationship with movement? If you're anything like me, for the first 30 years of my life, it was a problematic, on-again, off-again relationship, sort of like my college dating years ● I believed exercise and movement, intending to have a lower weight and healthier body, was a punishment. It seemed to me as though God had made me with a "bad metabolism," and the thin girls I knew he had "blessed" with a "good metabolism." While there are some truths to a genetic predisposition to weight and health, I was not honest about my lack of healthy movement or the frequent fast food and desserts I

Ross, J. (2002). The Mood Cure (1st ed.). Penguin Books.

consumed. I suffered from a lot of health issues, many of which stemmed from lethargy and heaviness, both physical and spiritual. My body was tired all the time. Even if I slept well at night, I needed naps to get through the day. I was spiritually heavy as well, with a consistent negative, tired, bummy feeling that surrounded me.

I shared in my introduction that the Lord delivered me from a spirit of heaviness, which had me bound since my dad died in 2002. I was heavy in my spirit. The Bible talks of the spirit of heaviness and the healing of Jesus that combats it. **"To console those who mourn in Zion, To give them beauty for ashes, The oil of joy for mourning, The garment of praise for the spirit of heaviness; That they may be called trees of righteousness, The planting of the Lord, that He may be glorified."** Isaiah 61:3 NKJV

Jesus brings the oil of joy for mourning and a garment of praise for the spirit of heaviness. This garment replaces the old, heavy one, and as the spirit of heaviness leaves, the righteousness of Christ abounds, and we become planted near living waters, able to glorify the King in all that we do. When I was living in a place of bondage, under such heaviness, I was too tired to be used by the Lord. I was depressed and full of grief, and it led me to stay in bed, to stay on the couch, literally in a dark house, for many days, for many years. I watched a lot of T.V. and spent a lot of time online 'numbing out,' and the last thing I ever wanted to do was to move my body or work out. The enemy uses this spirit of heaviness to get people tocome under such a feeling of defeat that they never even try. Do you know that feeling? It feels like losing weight or getting healthy seems like a pipe dream that will take SO much time and SO much effort, and where is the motivation to sustain it? Where is the time? Where is the energy?

Once again, much of my focus was on how I felt and not much on who God is and who he has called me to be. The end of that verse says, "That they may be called trees of righteousness, The planting of the Lord, that He may be glorified." Our "planting" in Christ allows Him to be glorified through everything we do as worship unto the Lord. As we live through Christ, he can work in many people's lives and use us in numerous ways. When I stayed rooted in the bed and rooted on the couch, I was not allowing myself to be available to the needs of others and to see God glorified through me. I thank God for his mercy and for healing me and delivering me. I love seeing people touched by the love of Jesus, and partnering with God means more to me than anything in this world.

Moving your body does not mean going to the gym and beating your body into submission for hours a day. It means you understand that your body is designed divinely to move and rest.

> "For in Him we live and move and exist [that is, in Him we actually have our being], as even some of your own poets have said, 'For we also are His children'."
> Acts 17:28 AMP

Your movement is not just exercise; it is being active in the kingdom. We can allow the Lord to minister to the world through us, and this is rarely achieved when we are just sitting at home day after day, night after night. Now, please hear my heart; I understand entirely some times and circumstances that require us to rest, and many people are not currently in a physical state that allows them to move or leave their homes. This teaching is to challenge those of us who, for different reasons, have allowed the weight of the world and the condemnation of the enemy to cause us to be ineffective, exhausted, and to suffer, leading us to stay in a place of stagnation.

Did you know just "20 minutes (of movement) can act as an anti-inflammatory"? What a fantastic built-in blessing! God designed us to move and, in that movement, to bless our bodies. Research has shown that just a few minutes of walking after a meal can help to decrease blood sugar immediately. The American Diabetes Association shared that a single round of exercise can lower blood sugar for up to 24 hours afterward, depending on the intensity and duration of the exercise. One study states that just 7½ minutes of high-intensity exercise may help to stabilize blood sugar from one to three days afterward.

Movement can be enjoyable and challenging in a healthy way. You can allow the Holy Spirit to use anything in your life to assist you in growing and stretching you to become more mature in your faith, content in all things, as Paul talks about in Phillippians. I

https://www.sciencedaily.com/releases/2017/01/170112115722.htm
https://www.eatingwell.com/article/7998411/walking-after-meals-lower-blood-sugar-science/
https://www.ncbi.nlm.nih.gov/pmc/articles/PMC3587394/

have learned through hard workouts that I can endure much more discomfort than I thought.

The Lord has been teaching me about the idol of comfort, particularly in my life and the American culture. We LOVE comfort in America. You can probably think of one commercial you've seen in the past month that uses the word comfort. We love "comfy" clothes, shoes, seats, couches, cars, beds, pillows, the list could go on and on. I am not saying that you cannot be comfortable; what I am saying is that you should challenge whether you allow comfort to supersede obedience. When God called me to write this book, it was uncomfortable. Talking about weight, diets, idols, and demons is not your everyday lighthearted subject matter, and it has a lot of hot-button emotions attached. If I were to have said, "Ok, God, I hear you; I know you want me to write this book, but it's just too uncomfortable," then I would have made comfort more important than obedience to God and, therefore, an idol. Sure, laying in bed and on the couch watching T.V. is way comfier and often more enjoyable, but is it producing Life in your life?

Once again, I am NOT saying you can never rest or watch T.V.; I am just challenging you to take inventory of how you spend your days. You don't have to set world records or become a 'gym rat.' We are focusing on being mentally, spiritually, and physically healthy.

Weightless

I encourage you to pray aloud and invite your heavenly Father into your dislike of movement. Invite Him into your fear of discomfort.

A prayer might sound like this: **"Father, I don't like movement, especially working out.** I don't like getting hot and sweaty and messing up my hair. I don't like feeling out of breath or having lots of people around seeing what I am doing. I don't like feeling like I have already failed before I start. I know this is an area I need to surrender to you. Please help me find a way to enjoy living, moving, and being in you. Please help me to honor my body as it is the temple of the Holy Spirit. I repent for any way that I have allowed comfort to become an idol in my life. I ask you to bring that idol down in Jesus' name. I ask that you help me become steadfast in my decisions and be firmly planted in you so you can use me in your kingdom. I desire to be whole and healthy in every way. Please show me how to worship you through everything that I do. I ask you to fill me with your Holy Spirit and help me to surrender to your will and your way for my life."

The Lie: It's All My Fault

Receiving the understanding that you are loved and never alone breaks off the lie that it is all your fault. I want you to grab a piece of paper and a pen. Would you start by praying this aloud: **"Father, would you reveal to me the lies that I have been believing about my body, food, and movement?"** Now, could you take a moment to let Him speak to you? Consider the lies that you have been partnering with and write them down.

The Lie Breaker

Read this prayer aloud with BOLDNESS! Step into the truth God has for you! Pray it daily, if needed. Take every thought captive- literally, grab the negative thoughts Satan spews at you and throw them out. Fill your heart with truth and hope from the Word.

"Father, I repent and walk away from the lies I have believed that do not line up with your truth. I repent and walk away from self-hatred. I repent and walk away from self-focus. I repent and walk away from the idol of comfort. I repent and walk away from the idol of food. I repent and walk away from (Fill in your own here) _____. I receive the forgiveness you bought for me on the cross. I choose to forgive myself for (whatever you still feel angry with yourself about) _____. I ask that you would come and heal the wounds on my soul and show me the truths that you want me to know. I receive your love, your light, and your glory. Amen."

Lie #3

"I'd be valuable if..."

You probably have not said this lie directly, but the phrase is a synopsis of how you have probably felt at some point in your life. Have you ever caught yourself saying things like "If I could just..." in reference to your success with a diet, your consistency with the gym, or your motivation? Have you found your thoughts drifting to how much better you'd feel about yourself if you could meet your goals? Then, you might be stuck in the lie that your value is based on your behavior and performance.

You aren't alone in that thinking. In American culture, most people freely talk about themselves in this way. I feel like I often hear more dialogue about the diet and exercise programs people are on or have fallen off of than the important and valuable things in their lives. This is probably because most of us have grown up believing that our value is hugely impacted by our body shape and size, how we dress, what car we drive, how big our house is...on and on. These superficial metrics are without purpose and leave people feeling small and empty. The following words dive into some of the different ways we fall into the trap of trying to do more to be valuable.

"If I could just stick to a diet..."

Growing up in the 90s, I couldn't watch TV without seeing ads for "low-fat" foods, Slimfast, and the South Beach Diet book. I remember my mom buying fat-free desserts and she was often found doing different diets like the cabbage soup diet, the cayenne lemon water diet, and I could go on and on. She, along with the rest of America was bombarded with the idea that to be beautiful is to be thin, and to be thin is to be beautiful.

I remember being on "a diet" as early as 14 years old. Thoughts about what I ate and what I looked like filled my mind from a very early age. This led to what I call the **Shame|Pride Cycle** in my life.

"WHEN WE ARE DRIVEN BY SELF-HATRED OR THE FEAR OF WHAT PEOPLE THINK ABOUT US, WE RUN ON A LIMITED MOTIVATION SUPPLY."

Shame/Pride Cycle

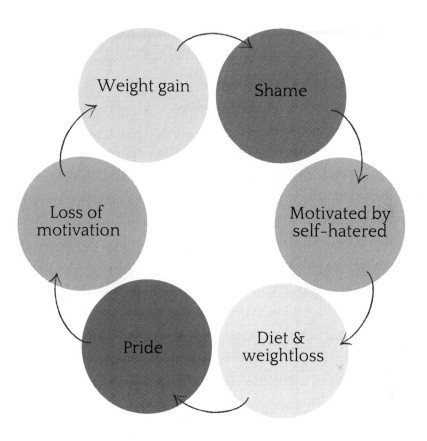

My life from high school on was a version of this cycle. While on a diet I felt strong, capable, proud and worthy of attention. I lost weight and suddenly felt prettier, and more valuable. I would be proud of what I had accomplished and for a time I would manage the weight. As life crept in I would lose motivation. I was motivated by self-hatred, disappointment in my self and the desire to be loved/seen as worthy. This motivation is not sustainable because it is based on self, and lies.

When we are driven by self-hatred or the fear of what people think about us, we run on a limited motivation supply. When it runs out, it runs out. When we are on empty and can no longer stay motivated, what happens? I always ended up gaining back all the weight I lost and I stepped back into a place of shame and guilt for "failing". This created the **Shame|Pride Cycle** I mentioned earlier,, which was always based on how I **felt** vs. **truth**. I could feel ugly, fat, worthless all day long but the truth is that I am valuable, beautiful, inside and out, and worth more than anything in this world.

Even though I had heard that I was beautiful and important from family and a few others in my life, the time I had spent believing that I was ugly and the amount of lies I heard on a regular basis prevented me from believing it to be true. How much of our culture rotates around beauty and looks is truly astounding. Growing up in an age where I didn't have a cell phone until I was 16, and even then, ALL it could do was make phone calls with a limited amount of minutes, I was spared what many young women today are enduring. Apps like TikTok, Snapchat, Instagram, and Facebook are all sources of pressure to look and act a certain way. The even wilder thing is the number of women online who have completely altered their physical appearance through AI and other apps that create "perfect" proportions and facial features, which leads many to feel like they can never measure up to the beauty standards. In my vocation as a mental health coach, I hear so many young women share about the pressures they face to look a certain way. Even younger women, 14-16 years old, seem to act and dress much older because of all they are exposed to. The pressures to be thin and perfect add up every day.

The Bible tells us pride comes before a fall, and I think of it in that way when I look at the **Shame|Pride Cycle**-falling into shame is a dark and lonely process that can leave you feeling lost, alone, and without hope. The enemy uses this to steal joy and his ultimate desire, to steal your faith. If he can get you in a place where you feel God has abandoned you and all you can hear is demonic lies whispering in your ears, then he can quickly get you to walk away from your faith in the only one who loves you completely, just as you are. **What lies have you heard whispering to you when you fall short of your goals?**

I often heard things like, "You're such a failure." "You always do this." "You will never be able to lose weight." "You're so lazy." These words and more plagued my mind when I fell away from my planned diet and when I was no longer losing weight. My mind was a playground for these horrible thoughts, and I had no idea how to make them stop. It was an exhausting process that made it even more challenging to desire to exercise, eat healthy, and meet my goals. I lived in a self-fulfilled prophecy of failure.

"If I could just exercise more..."

I used to see girls running outside or working out at the gym, and I felt so negative about their behavior. I felt like they had won the lottery and had superhuman willpower, motivation, and desire to work out. I thought I had been given the short straw and had no innate desire or motivation to exercise and move my body. I HATED working out. Even short walks in the woods or a neighborhood brought me anger and frustration. I could not stand the idea of HAVING to work out to lose weight.

Around 2018, I began to work out consistently. I began to learn that God made my body to move. Every body was designed intelligently by God to move! We can move through the power of Christ with or without intrinsic motivation or desire. After I wrapped my head around the idea that Christ, living in me, is the source of my movement and the way to my living. I began to fuel my workouts with worship. Instead of attempting to beat my body into looking a certain way, I now look forward to my workouts!! My husband laughs and says I "run circles around him now," which is a joke considering he was a professional athlete and I was a professional couch surfer for most of our marriage! I often pray as I work out. I send up whispers of praise to my God and thank him for the gift of movement. It has brought such a sweetness to my life. Now, I can do anything, walk anywhere, carry heavy things, and help others. I no longer feel constantly limited by my body, and I thank GOD!

How many times have you looked in the mirror and either thought or said aloud, "If I just worked out more..." or, "If I could just get motivated to go to the gym..." Thoughts like these drift in and appear harmless, don't they? It looks as though you desire an increase in motivation, healthy movement, and weight loss. But the typical root of those thoughts is a belief that your weight would be "ideal" if you could get your butt in the gym and stick to a consistent routine, right? So, what's wrong with that thought? The idea of consistently working out is nice, but the motivation behind it can be faulty and dangerous. Like most things in life, exercise is inherently neither good nor evil; however, add an unhealthy perception of self behind it as your motivation for movement and be prepared for disappointment. Why is this?

When we place the idea that "beating our bodies into submission" is beneficial, without understanding why, we begin to operate out of shame and an inherent dislike of our bodies instead of a place of worship to God and honor towards our bodies. In **1 Corinthians 9:25-27 TPT**, Paul uses a metaphor: **"A true athlete will be disciplined in every respect, practicing constant self-control to win a laurel wreath that quickly withers. But we run our race to win a victor's crown that will last forever. For that reason, I don't run just for exercise or box like one throwing aimless punches, but I train like a champion athlete. I subdue my body and get it under my control, so that after preaching the good news to others I myself won't be disqualified."** Paul explains that he was committed to bending his will to the will of the Holy Spirit- to subdue his desires to the desires of God so that he would not be operating in his flesh but in the Spirit.

When we go into situations with the idea that we need to perform or do for God or because we want an outcome that is inherently about us, we tend to miss out on the complete revelation. God wants our whole hearts attuned to Him and bonded in relationship with Him. He does not desire you to bend your desires to His out of a selfish need but out of deep, intimate love for you, knowing that His way is better and that He is working all things out for your good. When we realize that exercise and movement are built-in blessings for our bodies and are worship to our creator, the motivation changes. For example, look at these two scenarios:

Scenario One
Jill looks in the mirror and immediately focuses her eyes and attention on her shape and form. She stares at her not-flat stomach and feels frustration, guilt, and shame. She begins to think about all the food she's eaten that has led to the lack of weight loss, all the times she's skipped the gym. Thoughts begin to fill her head. "If I had just stopped with one chip instead of 20!" "My stomach wouldn't be this ugly if I had just been born with a better metabolism!" "This is all my fault." "I have to get to the gym ASAP."

Throughout this scenario, Jill has only focused on herself; her thoughts, looks, disappointment, and looking to herself for answers have left her feeling more discouraged and frustrated. The motivation source of discouragement and desire to change is limited and will not last long because it relies on negative feelings of self, which are not life-giving and will not fuel the motivation.

She will most likely give up because she feels her goal is impossible.

Scenario Two

Jill looks in the mirror and notices that she's gained some weight. She feels herself drifting towards negative thoughts about herself and recognizes that she needs to talk to God about it. So she begins to pray, **"Father, I notice I have gained some weight. I have been enjoying time with my family and friends, which led to a shift in my eating and time at the gym. I thank you, Lord, for providing me with rich experiences filled with the love of family and friends. I praise you, Lord, for my body, crafted in your image, filled with health, strength, vitality, and purpose. Thank you for teaching me your ways and for showing me how to fuel my body in a way that honors you. Will you fill me with a desire to honor my body with the food I eat? Will you increase my desire to worship you through movement? Please help me steward my body well and honor it with my words and thoughts. Take my thoughts off of myself and keep my mind stayed on you. I repent for partnering with lies about my body. I bind every negative thought about my body in the name of Jesus and release the truth that I am wonderfully made, in the image of God and that I can do all things, through Christ who strengthens me."**

In this scenario, Jill recognizes that she has had a change in her body, eating, and exercise, but she turns her focus from self and self-image to God and his image, answers, and strength. The source of motivation is unlimited because the source is the worship of God and receiving His power in her weakness.

One of the things I have learned about myself in the journey to enjoying movement is that I get bored with workouts! I started exercising consistently around 2019 with an online program. The program was a weightlifting and HIIT-focused circuit that changed each day. However, there were only a set number of videos and exercises, and I began to get tired of the same old thing week after week. In June of 2021, one of my best friends, Amber, talked me into going with her to her gym, Twisted Cycle. Even the name sounded intimidating! I went into my first workout feeling overwhelmed and even said, "I hate that class." It was challenging and tiring, and I felt I couldn't keep up. But I had signed up for the free week pass and was determined to try again. By the end of the week, I was loving it! I loved the challenge of the workouts, and I felt stronger. My husband had already signed up for a membership, and we were able to exercise together. It has become a date night of sorts for us. It is still a challenging workout, and there are times that I need to modify and adjust the exercises (I can't do a pullup, yet!), but I have grown in strength in my body and my mind. There are times during a particularly challenging workout that I begin to pray; I thank God for the gift of my health and for the ability to move and grow.

"If I could just stay motivated."

I don't know about you, but I can't count how many resolutions I have made to lose weight, keep the house clean, stretch more, watch my carbs, the list could go on and on and on. I have often started the new year with fresh motivation as if the slate has been wiped clean, and I am a new person with a new reason to keep my resolutions. I have even been able to run on that motivation for a while, keeping up with my goals for a time, but every year, I see them slipping after 2 or 3 months. **Why is that??** I believe it is because we are often motivated by the result we desire, not the nature of completeness we already live in. What does that mean you ask? When I used to begin a resolution to lose weight, my motivation was to lose weight; it might also be to be healthier or feel better about myself. All of these motivations are driven by myself, by my flesh. So, the only way I can succeed in these motivations is to keep looking at myself, typically negatively, and getting inspiration through my self.

Self-hatred was my primary source of fuel. See how that might fail after a while? My self is not the source of answers or motivation; Christ in me provides the source of all I need. The source is Holy Spirit, creative genius, comforter, guide, and friend. When I look within and see Christ, and I realize that perfect love has cast out fear and provided **Shalom**- which means **nothing missing, nothing broken, nothing lacking**- I know that I can begin to apply the true love of Christ to my life, even to myself, and there I begin to see things shift. My motivation in everything changes to the fact that I am a child of God, an heir, and can do ALL things through Christ, who strengthens me!

This motivation carries me when my self-starter mentality fails, when the days come that I don't want to work out, or when I decide to eat the fries! I remember that these are momentary choices and are not decisions that derail my purpose of living in a way that honors my body as a living sacrifice. It all boils down to the reality of Christ living in and through me. This takes away the striving, the pressure, and the anxiety and gives me breathing room. As the verse below states, I am ready for anything because I live in Christ's sufficiency instead of relying on my feeble humanity.

I can do all things [which He has called me to do] through Him who strengthens and empowers me [to fulfill His purpose—I am self-sufficient in Christ's sufficiency; I am ready for anything and equal to anything through Him who infuses me with inner strength and confident peace.]
Philippians 4:13 AMP

I invite you to join me in the rest-filled life, even on the days when it feels anything but restful! Christ, the hope of Glory lives in you and will help you not only endure hardships but get moving and bless your body as you eat, sleep, etc. He cares about what you care about. Invite him into the little things. Ask him "Lord, what type of movement should I try today?" "Will this food bless my body?" He will answer. Give him time and space to respond. He loves all of you, so very much.

The Lie: "I'd Be Valuable If..."

When we seek to find value in sources outside of the inherited, unshakeable value God has given us, we end up wanting. We will continue on and on in whatever way possible, trying to prove to ourselves and others that we are valuable, and we will be led astray, time after time. True value lies on the cross and all that Christ did for us. The Father has adopted us, calling us His own, bringing us into a relationship with Him, and restoring our identity. We must partner with Him in this truth and break agreement with the pervasive lies. Let's do that together...

The Lie Breaker

Pray aloud with me:

"Lord, I repent for agreeing with the lie that I have to maintain my behaviors to be successful and receive my value from those things. I break off all words I have spoken that aligned with that lie and receive the truth that my value is detached from my behavior. I receive the truth that my value is in Christ alone. I receive the truth that my value was established before the earth's foundations, as I am your creation. Lord, I ask that you reveal your love for me and show me how my value is established in you alone. I ask you to build a holy strength in me to be able to do what you have called me to do. I choose to build my life on you alone and not on anything I try to do in my own strength. Thank you for your love and grace. Amen."

Lie #4
"I'm Not Worth the effort."

I have already shared a lot about how thoughts of unworthiness, self-hatred, and doubt lead us to think that we are unloved, leading to a loss of motivation. I want to add to this topic by sharing how the enemy creeps in and uses undesirable circumstances to make us feel as though we are not worthy of the effort to receive wholeness. **Revelation 12:10 AMP** mentions Satan as **"...the accuser of our brothers and sisters..."**. Satan and his evil minions do not desire that you live in fullness; instead, they accuse you and keep you bound up in self-hatred, self-pity, and self-loathing. These emotions focus on the self and keep you wholly bound and ineffectual in being a vessel of victory for those around you. Here's the thing Satan doesn't want you to know: **when you receive true freedom and healing and live in wholeness, you will live your entire life differently. You will live on purpose in all you do.**

I used to walk into rooms and feel immediately less than. I would think about how my stomach roll looked while I sat in my chair and how lucky so-and-so was sitting across from me because she could eat whatever she wanted and not gain a pound. After being set free through Jesus, I now walk into rooms with my head up, not in pride, but in confidence, free from shame. I know that anything good, pure, lovely, or righteous seen in me is the work of Holy Spirit in my life. I walk into rooms thinking of people I can bless, encourage, and love. I walk in, eager to practice listening to God's voice to share His hope, love, joy, and the possibility that they can live a victorious life through Him.

Adoption

One of the ways that I began to walk in His victory was by learning that I am adopted into the family of God. **Ephesians 1:5-6 TPT "For it was always in his perfect plan to adopt us as his delightful children, through our union with Jesus, the Anointed One, so that his tremendous love that cascades over us would glorify his grace—for the same love he has for his Beloved One, Jesus, he has for us. And this unfolding plan brings him great pleasure!"** Romans 8:15-16 ESV says, "You did not receive the spirit of slavery to fall back into fear, but you have received the Spirit of adoption as sons, by whom we cry, "Abba! Father!" The Spirit himself bears witness with our spirit that we are children of God."

When Paul used this analogy of adoption during Roman times, it was well known to his audience that adoption was a very serious and significant act in many ways more meaningful than being a natural-born heir. In the Roman world, adoption was a significant and common practice...These adoptions were not infant adoptions as is common today. Typically Older boys and adult men were adopted...When the adoption was legally approved, the adoptee would have all his debts canceled, and he would receive a new name. He would be the legal son of his adoptive father and entitled to all the rights and benefits of a son. A father could disown his natural-born son, but adoption was irreversible. **Adoption as a child of God is irreversible!** Is that not amazing?! I love that I have been grafted into the lineage of Jesus!

Our Father has always planned for us to be adopted and brought into his family. The death of Jesus was our birthday! He never desired that we would live separately from him, and he placed a plan of redemption from the foundation of the world. It brings me to tears when I think of the truth that I am a daughter of God Almighty. His love for me is boundless, and he does not desire that I live in bondage to anything. If I was worth Jesus' effort to come live amongst humans and die by their hand, how then can I live a life believing that I am not worthy of receiving freedom in my body, soul, and spirit to live in that freedom he bought? The awareness of my worth to Christ drives me to gratitude, pulls me into His embrace, and makes me desire to bless Him in all I do. It also removes the pressure to perform.

Words of Life or Words of Death

When God began to take me on a journey of healing regarding the way I saw myself, he began to highlight the fact that I was constantly speaking words of "death" over myself. I struggled to succeed and felt like I would fail because I often told myself I would fail. I'd say, "I probably shouldn't join a gym; I'll stop going after a week, anyway."

I would speak "death" over situations before I ever even tried to do something. And the root of that was fear. I was afraid of failing, and honestly, I was even scared to succeed. I've shared it already, but **Proverbs 18:21 AMP** reminds us, **"Death and life are in the power of the tongue, and those who love it and indulge it will eat its fruit and bear the consequences of their words."** In the past, I bore the consequences of my words. I would often say things to friends like "I look so fat..." to try to get ahead of them thinking that about me. I had a faulty belief that I needed to speak out about the negatives so that people couldn't think of them for me. It was a strange "ownership" of the curses I was speaking, and I believe the enemy used them to keep me in bondage. It caused me to bear the fruit of my own words.

During this time in my life, I had so much inflammation in my body, and I know that it directly correlated to how I thought and spoke about my body. I would look in the mirror and loathe what I saw. I would weep looking at my form, feeling physically sick to my stomach, thinking about how ugly I looked. I would get so angry at myself for not sticking to my plans of dieting and exercise, for failing again and again. I held unforgiveness and bitterness towards myself and my body. Your body has the ability to hold the memory of experiences, trauma, and the words spoken about and to it. There are so many scriptures that line up with this teaching.

Prov 23:7 AMP: "For as he thinks in his heart, so is he..."

James 3:5-6, 8 TPT: "And so the tongue is a small part of the body yet it carries great power! Just think of how a small flame can set a huge forest ablaze. And the tongue is a fire! It can be compared to the sum total of wickedness and is the most dangerous part of our human body. It corrupts the entire body and is a hellish flame! It releases a fire that can burn throughout the course of human existence...but the tongue is not able to be tamed. It's a fickle, unrestrained evil that spews out words full of toxic poison!"

Proverbs 18:8 AMP "The words of a whisperer (gossip) are like dainty morsels [to be greedily eaten]; They go down into the innermost chambers of the body [to be remembered and mused upon]."

In Hebrew, the word for a whisperer, or gossiper, is **nirgân**, which means to murmur, whisper: murmurer, backbiter, slanderer, talebearer. Have you been slandering and backbiting yourself? Proverbs tells us that the words go down into the innermost chambers of the body, into the belly. The word for belly in Hebrew is **beṭenan** and describes the belly, womb, and abdomen.

When we speak slanderous, backbiting words over ourselves, the body receives them and "remembers and muses upon" them. You can probably personally attest to this. **Let's pause here.** Can you think of a time you were arguing with someone you love, and they spoke such harsh words over you that you could feel them land in your physical body? Depending on the severity of that situation and whether you have released and received forgiveness in that memory or not, you might still feel it in your body now. I want you to think back on those words you heard, or spoke over yourself, that moment, that argument, and the emotions that came up as you thought about it.

Can you remember who spoke the words that hurt you?
What was said?
How did you feel?
Do you know where in your body those words landed? In your heart (chest), in your stomach? Somewhere else?

Please take a moment and allow Holy Spirit to reveal those memories. I encourage you to write them down. It might take a moment or it could take hours. Lean in to the Lord and his desire to heal you.

You might also use the following prayer to guide you in prayer for the words of death you or others have spoken over yourself:

Pray aloud with me:
"Holy Spirit, I ask you to come right now and help me to accept your love and forgiveness over this situation. I choose to forgive _____ (Name the person(s) who hurt you) for _____ (What they did). I forgive them for being used by the enemy to hurt me. I repent for judging them. I tear up every debt, and I bless them, in Jesus' name. I give you _____ (the emotion(s) you felt), and I ask you to take these emotions from me. I ask Holy Spirit that you would come into my _____ (Place you feel the pain) and bring healing. I ask you to heal the wounds on my soul and bring me peace. Would you fill me up again and train my tongue to bring blessings instead of curses? Train me to hear your voice above all others. "

Fear of Failure

In the past, whenever I thought about the coming New Year, I would begin to fantasize about how I could look that Summer if I started working out on January 1st. I would buy a new planner and calendar and write out goals, weight loss always being #1. I would plan out my meals and buy all the veggies and fruits. I began with such high hopes and ideals, but soon, things came along that made it much harder to accomplish my goals. I'd get an invite to a birthday party and be unable to say no to the cake. Then, a few days later, there would be a dessert at home, and friends would want pizza. It goes on and on. You know the story; you start off well, then life happens, and you fall off the wagon. My problem was when I 'fell off the wagon,' I stayed on the ground. When I fell, I just sat on the ground and became stuck. Those lies took up their tools and built walls, a floor and a roof around me, and I became their prisoner. My value was so connected to the outcome of weight loss that I honestly had no identity. I began to eat more and more, and I stopped working out. My weight crept up, and depression set in. I was also entirely oppressed by the enemy. Those lies I mentioned weren't just little thoughts I came up with but, indeed, demonic voices that attached to my ears, cursing me night and day. I was heavy, both physically and spiritually. It felt like I would never be free.

As time went by, I felt like I was not worthy of the time and effort it would take to implement the changes my health needed. Those oppressive thoughts kept me bound, and as I meditated on those negative thoughts, I stayed in bondage. Whatever we think about, we typically do.

Have you experienced one of these negative thought loops? I see it as a swirl, like a cyclone... It starts as a thought, then grows in size and length and continues swirling around you, often causing paralysis and keeping you stuck. The thought swirl is destructive and can quickly 'take territory' in your mind and life. The verse **"And do not be conformed to this world [any longer with its superficial values and customs], but be transformed and progressively changed [as you mature spiritually] by the renewing of your mind" Romans 12:2 AMP** reminds us that our minds cannot be renewed by anything but the word and truth of Jesus Christ. You also cannot stay in a place of anxiety and worry while you are filling your mind and your lips with gratitude. An Italian study found that gratitude reduces the overall effect of anxiety and depression in individuals studied.

https://www.psychologytoday.com/us/blog/comfort-gratitude/202012/gratitude-protects-against-depression

"Finally, believers, whatever is true, whatever is honorable and worthy of respect, whatever is right and confirmed by God's word, whatever is pure and wholesome, whatever is lovely and brings peace, whatever is admirable and of good repute; if there is any excellence, if there is anything worthy of praise, think continually on these things [center your mind on them, and implant them in your heart]."
Philippians 4:8 AMP

When you begin to sense a thought swirl coming along, take that thought captive- reach out and grab it. Examine that thought as if you could see it. Does it line up with the truth of God's word? Does it line up with the work of the cross? Does it line up with God's heart for you? If you aren't sure, I recommend marinating on the following verses and searching out the truth in God's word for yourself because He has already given us "Everything we could ever need for life and godliness..."2 Peter 1:3 TPT.

James 1:17 TPT: "Every gift God freely gives us is good and perfect, streaming down from the Father of lights, who shines from the heavens with no hidden shadow or darkness and is never subject to change."

Psalms 139:14 TPT: "I thank you, God, for making me so mysteriously complex! Everything you do is marvelously breathtaking. It simply amazes me to think about it! How thoroughly you know me, Lord!"

I often thought my value was conditional, based on my size, whether I met my weight loss goals, or "feeling" pretty enough. This value system I created had nothing to do with my value as a daughter of God. Just yesterday, I spoke with a friend, and she pointed out that we often value ourselves in every way but how God has valued us. So, it makes sense that we feel like we are not worth the time or effort to succeed at what we put our hands to. **If you think you are a failure before you begin, does it not stand to reason that you will likely fail?**

Fear of Success

Have you ever gotten over the hump of failure and began to get close to your goal and start to feel fearful? I certainly have. Many times in my journey, I began to lose weight, and I could see my goal weight nearing me. I would start feeling afraid and even find myself self-sabotaging- eating more off plan because I had already reached enough of my goal- gaining some weight just before I achieved my goal. It was as if I feared what I would find on the other side of the destination.

On one side, we have the trap of the enemy that we are not worthy of the effort to succeed; on the other side, we have the trap that we are not worthy of the success we achieve. We begin to fear failure and success. **If you put your worth and value in the outcome, then you will never be truly free to enjoy the victory of that outcome.** When the goal or outcome becomes your life's purpose instead of a part of your purpose, you will never be able to truly live in freedom, even if you reach the destination. You will begin to fear losing the goal (in my case, it would be weight gain after meeting my weight loss goal).

Over the past year, my weight has fluctuated from the goal. I gained a dress size from my lowest weight loss, and it was tough. There were days when I felt like such a failure. I felt I had lost my motivation. In reality, my body is just fluctuating. I have had a hectic year, traveling more than I ever have, which means not eating at home as much and not being able to work out as much. I talked to my husband about it a few months ago, and he said, "Jill, your body is not a robot; it will not always be exactly the same." That gave me such a sweet perspective and caused me to pause and reflect on why I was so bothered by the changes I saw. I realized that if my worth is based on my body's appearance or dress size, I have completely missed my actual value.

The cross is my valuation.
To Jesus, I was worth his life.
I am still worth it to Him.
To idolize the scale or dress size is a sin.
It is in direct conflict with God's heart, and it is what he died to free us from. We are worth so much more than how we look. We are worth Jesus' life and love. It can be hard to wrap our heads around that selfless, pure love. It is so holy, and it enfolds us in righteousness.

The Lie: "I'm Not Worth the Effort."

God has brought conviction as He has shown me how thoughts about my size have ruled me. He has shown me that these thoughts have often taken me captive and kept me in bondage. I have repented of placing my worth outside of truth. Would you like to join me?

The Lie Breaker

Pray aloud with me:

"Jesus, I repent for placing my value in my size, weight goals, looks, relationships, and _____ (fill in the blank). I repent for idolizing anything that is not you. I sever any words I have made in partnership with the lie that says I am only worthy if I meet and maintain my goals. I receive the truth that I am fearfully and wonderfully made, complete, and lacking nothing. I receive my worth from your death on the cross and apply your freedom to my body, soul, and spirit. Thank you for loving me unconditionally. Help me to love myself as you do. Amen."

You can repeat this prayer and flow with the Lord in prayer as other thoughts emerge.

Lie #5

"Love is All You Need."

I spent most of my life desiring to be loved. I thought about, dreamed about, and wrote about love. I was full of romantic notions of a guy coming to sweep me off my feet who would tell me how beautiful I was and heal my broken heart. I was waiting to be approved. I often felt like I could only make decisions once this guy came and brought about my life's purpose through marriage. Maybe you have walked a similar road, feeling that true love would heal you and bring you value. True love cannot come through a man, but the man Jesus. Jesus is the only true lover of your soul.

In the following pages, I have shared how this idea that love heals manipulates your heart to steal your joy, peace, and identity. We cannot receive healing until we receive true LOVE Himself.

The Love of Marriage

As a child, my dad often laid his hand on my head at night and prayed a 'Father's Blessing' over me. He would pray for sweet sleep, health, strength, peace, etc., and he often prayed for my future spouse and their family. I grew up expecting to marry a loving husband who would fit the missing space I had in me. My mom and dad had a good relationship and were always very affectionate with one another. They were both committed Christians dedicated to making their marriage a healthy one, which included date nights EVERY Saturday night, which meant I became their built-in babysitter as soon as I was legally old enough ● As much as I disliked babysitting my little brothers, I love that my parents never stopped dating each other. They often kissed, danced, sang together, and enjoyed life as one.

As a kid, I often fantasized about my wedding day, draping curtains over my head to make a veil and holding my mom's dried flowers as my bouquet. I loved dressing my Barbies in their wedding attire and often arranged their weddings! I grew up in a house that focused on being pure and waiting until marriage for sex. There was never a conversation about being single; it was just a given that I would be married. So, my thoughts always focused on being married.

After receiving a purity ring from my parents, I began writing letters to my future husband when I was 13. The ring was to sit on my ring finger as a reminder to remain pure until my future husband replaced it with a ring on my engagement day. Looking back, I believe my parents had lovely intentions, but the focus on marriage was limiting. What if I had never married? Would I be somehow less than? I believe the American Christian church has put a significant emphasis on marriage to assist young people in remaining pure, but what about the many who never "find the right one" or who are called to singleness? I have learned that to be genuinely pure is not just to abstain from sex but to live with a heart posture of purity. This means to die daily to your desires. It is to love the Lord with all your heart, soul, mind, and strength; to love Him with your whole being and consecrate it (set it apart) for His glory and purposes. We give up all fleshly desires, not just sex. Marriage is not our savior. It does not create purity in the mind, spirit, and heart. To say that is to idolize marriage and to put it in Jesus' place, which is something that I did for years.

As the years progressed, I began to build an idea of my future husband and even created a list that included a musician, cute, funny, fun, taller than me, makes me laugh, a tender loving heart, friend, and more. As I started liking boys, I quickly learned that not all boys liked me. I was not everyone's ideal. With each rejection from a boy, self-doubt settled in more profoundly, and that self-doubt quickly became self-hatred.

"TO BE GENUINELY PURE IS NOT JUST TO ABSTAIN FROM SEX BUT TO LIVE WITH A HEART POSTURE OF PURITY. THIS MEANS TO DIE DAILY TO YOUR DESIRES."

In college, I filled my prayer journal entries with the hope I had found "the one," and then pages literally stained with tears when boys told me they "just want to be friends" or they started dating someone else. Entries like this fill the pages of my journals along with actual tear stains, marking moments of my deep sadness and loneliness. I often slipped into depression as I sat pondering how long I would be alone.

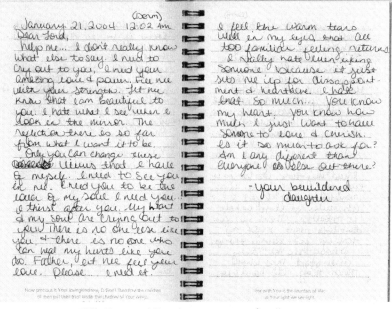

Jill's Journal Freshman year of college.

I truly believed a guy would come along and fill the broken places and help me believe I was enough. Do you see what I mean about idolizing marriage? This is what it looked like in my life: I put a guy in Jesus' place and allowed hopelessness and despair to come in and eat away at my peace and joy. I did not let Jesus have all of my heart because I kept a part of it hidden away for my husband, thinking that only he could heal it.

You've probably heard the phrase "he/she completes me" in a movie or conversation. This thinking leads to a massive imbalance in our lives as we rely on another person to be whole. That is so dangerous because humans are fallible and unpredictable. This way of thinking leads to emptiness, and that emptiness often turns to depression, bitterness, and an overall sense of "waiting" for life to start.

For those called to marriage, we were never created to be completed by another person. The Bible tells us, **"For this reason a man shall leave his father and his mother, and shall be joined to his wife; and they shall become one flesh." Genesis 2:24 AMP**. Becoming one flesh is speaking of the unity of marriage, the oneness established through covenant. It is not saying two halves come and make a whole, but that two whole people unify to create a new life and journey with God. This unity mirrors the union of the Trinity, one God in three parts, moving perfectly in harmony.

For many years I dreamed of a morning when I would wake up and love myself. I envisioned myself in wholeness, but I falsely believed that I would be healed by my husband loving and encouraging me enough. I placed a MASSIVE expectation on his shoulders to be my 'healer.' Once again, I put him in Jesus' position. I did not yet understand that Jesus was already my complete healer and that he had restored me fully; I just needed to accept that restoration and partner with its truth in my words. I know I have mentioned it already, but **Proverbs 18:21 AMP says, "Death and life are in the power of the tongue, And those who love it and indulge it will eat its**

fruit and bear the consequences of their words." We can thrive or suffer based on how we speak. I don't mean if you say aloud, "I'm going to receive one billion dollars" every day that, you will receive it, but I do mean that if you speak the truth of the Word of God over yourself, you will reap its blessings. Alternately, if you speak the lies the accuser says about you, you will reap their suffering.

The Love of Self

Over the past few years, I have seen a massive increase in phrases like "Self-care," "self-love," "Owning your truth," etc.... The idea is that no one can love you like you love yourself and that you need to foster self-care, i.e., taking care of yourself via pampering, boundary building, time doing what you love, making choices based on how you feel, and always "following your truth." While loving yourself and caring for yourself is not wrong, it can quickly become unhealthy and un-Biblical if not formed from God's Word.

Biblical self-love is often the opposite of the world's view of self-love. The Bible speaks about loving oneself, but not in a way that promotes self-centeredness or selfishness. Instead, Biblical self-love comes from the true knowledge and understanding of our identity as children of God. We love because he first loved us. He made us in his image; his word teaches us how to live in and through his love for us. Biblical self-love teaches us to care for ourselves in a way that aligns with God and his heart, not just around ur needs and wants. Jesus taught that you must love yourself; he said, **"And the second (commandment) is this: 'You must love your neighbor in the same way you love yourself.' You will never find a greater commandment than these."** Mark 12:31 TPT How can we love our neighbor if we do not first love ourselves? But the Bible also teaches that we must "die to ourselves." Galatians teaches us to **"Keep in mind that we who belong to Jesus Christ have already experienced crucifixion. For everything connected with our self-life was put to death on the cross and crucified with Messiah."** Galatians 5:24 TPT, so what does that mean regarding self-love? We are called to love ourselves as Christ loves us. **Romans 5:8 TPT** says, **"But Christ proved God's passionate love for us by dying in our place while we were still lost and ungodly!"**

When we were undeserving and truly lost, He died for us to return us to a place of right standing with Christ. When God, our Father, looks at us, He sees Jesus. He does not see your past, present mess, or future mistakes. He sees the righteousness of Jesus in you because Christ died to set you free! All the self-love in the world cannot obtain the true love and peace we receive through Jesus. In Christ, we are redeemed, righteous, and worthy of love. We are made perfect in love. We don't focus on the things of this mortal world and work to love ourselves. If we could obtain true love through our actions and words, we would not need Jesus and his sacrifice!

Alternatively, loving yourself just as you are, with the idea that you inherently know what's best for yourself and that within you can find the answers to all of life's estions will lead you down a deceptive and dark path.

Ezekiel 28:17 discusses how pride and arrogance led to Satan's downfall, **"Your heart was proud and arrogant because of your beauty; You destroyed your wisdom for the sake of your splendor. I cast you to the ground; I lay you before kings, That they might look at you."** The Bible shows us how the love of self and the arrogance and pride of the heart goes before the fall- which was literal for Lucifer as he believed that he was equal to God. This belief caused him to be thrown out of heaven. Pride masks itself in many ways, often in light and "love."

When we attempt to love ourselves from a place of self-love only, we begin to idolize ourselves. "Looking within" sounds innocent, like contemplation and self-examination. Still, this terminology is adopted by many in new age circles as they attempt to tap into much darker ideologies, such as the 'goddess within,' 'divine consciousness' and other beliefs that elicit the idea that all people are god-like and are connected to 'the divine' and that they must search within to find this god-like state. These are demonic ideologies that trap people into believing that their self is the answer to all things. Once again, the doctrine is self-motivated and focused but wrapped in terms of light **2 Corinthians 11:14 AMP** states that *"...Satan himself masquerades as an angel of light."*

I don't know about you, but I do not want to look within for answers and motivation in my life. Even on my best day, I know, **"The heart is deceitful above all things and it is extremely sick; Who can understand it fully and know its secret motives?"** Jeremiah 17:9 AMP.

Have you ever asked your heavenly Father, "Why do you love me?" and then waited for Him to answer? It is an amazing gift to allow the Father the space to speak His love over you. Would you stop now and pray this prayer and **wait** for Him to answer? Be still and know that he is with you and that He desires to speak to you. You might here a word in your heart or mind- likely something you would not say on your own. You could hear an audible voice! Wait and see. You might want a pen and paper nearby to write down what He says to you.

"Father, I want to hear clearly from you and you alone. Please guard my mind and ears from every lying voice. Will you speak to me now? Why do you love me?"

How was that experience? Was it new for you? Is it something you would be willing to start practicing? Many of us long to be loved but, we must learn WHO love is. We see Love written through the pages throughout scripture- even the Old Testament. God's love for His people began when He spoke life into the void. It continued as Adam and Eve willfully disobeyed Him. Have you ever considered that scenario when Adam and Eve ate the fruit? The Most High, The Holy One, did not wipe them off the planet after they sinned but immediately looked for them, calling out their names. He did not change their names or eradicate them; he found them and made a way for them to clothe themselves and to find a way back to Him through sacrifice. LOVE found a way to be restored in their hearts. His passionate love continues throughout His word and continues today as Holy Spirit meets you in your home and heart. God IS LOVE, and therefore, all

Love is birthed through Him. We can't fabricate it on our own, even though Hollywood and love songs try. The source of His love is HIM. When we seek HIM, we receive the most genuine love we could ever know, and out of that comes an abundance of love, mercy, and kindness toward ourselves and others. How can we have anything but true thoughts of love and appreciation for ourselves and our bodies when we realize that GOD himself sent His Son to DIE just for us... You are so valuable that Christ chose to sacrifice himself Just. For. You. **Romans 5:8 TPT "But Christ proved God's passionate love for us by dying in our place while we were still lost and ungodly!"**

The enemy will often take a truth like **Phillippians 2:3-4 AMP "Do nothing from selfishness or empty conceit [through factional motives, or strife], but with [an attitude of] humility [being neither arrogant nor self-righteous], regard others as more important than yourselves. Do not merely look out for your own personal interests, but also for the interests of others,"** and turn it into a lie. Many believers slip into the mentality that they must care for those around them, attending to their needs before their own, which can lead to exhaustion, resentment, and burnout. Did you catch verse 4? **"...do not MERELY look out for your own personal interest, but also for the interests of others."** The author points out that you should be looking out for yourself, just not ONLY for yourself. The issues at hand are not behavioral but matters of the heart.

Jesus himself set the example of Biblical self-care. He often went away to be with His Father. These times away brought Him refreshing, strengthening, and giving Him the 'manna' He needed to continue serving God's people. We are often so focused on the optics and responsibilities of caring for others that we miss out on the heart behind WHY we are caring for others. I have always been a "people person" and have loved being around people. I am often energized just by being in the presence of others and hearing their stories. In the past, I was usually found helping others, often to the detriment of my other responsibilities, including keeping my house in order and honoring time with my husband. I felt I was honoring God by serving others and "being there for them" when they needed someone.

In 2018, my love of people began to change. Suddenly, I became irritated by others; I became short-fused around them. At that time, I served on a women's retreat weekend and attended meetings leading up to the weekend. Each meeting felt tiresome, and I dreaded attending. I was overwhelmed just being in the large gathering, and all I wanted was to go home. During one meeting, I sat on the church pew and silently asked God, "Why do I feel this way? I don't even know who I am..." I heard His gentle response in my spirit, saying, "I am burning away your flesh, and it isn't going to feel good. I am removing your need for the approval of others, and will place in you my love for them, instead."

This gentle response led to nearly a year of processing through the real reasons I was so quick to assist others, why I needed to be seen as "good," "helpful," and "kind." I was receiving my identity in how people thought of me, not performing acts of love out of the love I had received in Christ. That time was difficult and isolating. At a Christmas party that year I remember hiding away from people in any space I could. My husband chastised me, saying, "You're being so rude!" I'm sure it appeared that way, but the pendulum had swung from one side to the other. I was being taken into a new place in my walk with God, but my soul (Mind, Will, and Emotions) had to be reframed to the truth. That time with God changed absolutely everything about my life. He began to teach me about Himself, and He revealed to me His heart and His love for me. When God opens up your eyes to see and your ears to truly hear, it is like nothing you've ever known. Suddenly, things you have heard your entire life begin to make sense, and your heart begins to connect to Him in ways you didn't think possible.

"I keep asking that the God of our Lord Jesus Christ, the glorious Father, may give you the Spirit of wisdom and revelation, so that you may know him better. I pray that the eyes of your heart may be enlightened in order that you may know the hope to which he has called you, the riches of his glorious inheritance in his holy people" Ephesians 1:17-18 AMP

As God aligns our eyes and ears to His, we will begin to see and hear like he does. We receive the understanding that everything we do is to glorify God. That means we live as surrendered vessels, not seeking to please ourselves but Him. When we live out of this place, we can love and serve others with a pure heart, without motivation for selfish gain in any capacity.

We are called to love others as Christ has loved us and our neighbors as ourselves. So, God has a built-in mechanism for us to love ourselves well! He desires that we know Him intimately so that we can love all of His creation well, ourselves included. When we love ourselves as He loved us, we receive the overflow of His love through our actions. What does this look like? It looks like receiving and giving yourself grace. It looks like being patient with your flaws and failings. It looks like speaking words of love and life over yourself. It looks like honoring your body in every action, whether moving your body or eating foods that will bless it. It means ensuring your needs are met, knowing that God will supply them all. The most amazing thing you can do for your own "Self-care" is to know your Father. Time spent reading His Word, meditating on Him, worshiping Him, and praying will bring you into deeper intimacy with Him. This time will increase your understanding of how priceless you are to Him. This knowledge builds your self-worth more than any self-help book ever could.

"THE MOST AMAZING THING YOU CAN DO FOR YOUR OWN "SELF-CARE" IS TO KNOW YOUR FATHER. "

The Love of Christ

As I shared earlier, my desire to be married began after seeing a beautiful marriage in my home. I know that my childhood experience is a rare one. To have Christian parents who valued Christ in their marriage above everything else is an incredible gift, and I know it taught me so much about living my life in a relationship with Jesus. Suppose you did not grow up in a Christian home with parents dedicated to one another, or perhaps your marriage has been without intimacy, faithfulness, and joy. In that case, it might be hard to picture pure intimacy with Jesus. The Trinity is an example of perfect unity that teaches us how to become one with Christ and one with one another as the body of Christ.

John 17:22-23 TPT explains the Trinity's unity and our call to join it saying, **"For the very glory you have given to me I have given them so that they will be joined together as one and experience the same unity that we enjoy. You live fully in me and now I live fully in them so that they will experience perfect unity, and the world will be convinced that you have sent me, for they will see that you love each one of them with the same passionate love that you have for me."** Jesus came to bring a unification to us that goes beyond just getting into heaven one day; it begins here and now in perfect unity with the Father, Son, and Holy Spirit. He called us to come into His marvelous light and receive the JOY of salvation life with Him.

When I was young, I was saved nearly every week. I would sit on the front row of our church and hear how I needed Jesus and His salvation power to keep me from hell and to be set free from my sins. I didn't understand that a true and abiding relationship keeps me in intimacy with Jesus, which draws me out of darkness and away from sin. So, most weeks I spent making mistakes as most kids do, and then on Sunday, a great and terrible fear would fill me, and I would be afraid after hearing, "If you died tonight, do you know where you are going???" I would run to the altar and kneel on the steps, face in my hands, asking Jesus to come into my heart and save me and keep me from hell.

This scenario repeated for years. In the meantime, no one seemed to notice a little girl fraught with anxiety and terror regarding the rapture and where I would go if I died. I understand the altar call and its importance, but the teaching lacked the fundamental element of LIVING OUT your salvation. I did not learn that you can live in a relationship with Jesus and be free of consistent sin cycles by His drawing power. **"If you remain in Me and My words remain in you [that is, if we are vitally united and My message lives in your heart], ask whatever you wish and it will be done for you"** John 15:7 AMP. God created us to live on the Word of God. It is the only thing in our world that will never fail. If you constantly speak negatively about yourself, you will likely continue to feel negatively about yourself. No other human on earth-not even the most well-intending husband will be able to break you free from the lies you are believing and speaking over yourself.

Only Jesus can break these words off of your life. Jesus is always speaking a better and final word over you. **Romans 8:34 NIV** says, **"Who then is the one who condemns? No one. Christ Jesus who died—more than that, who was raised to life—is at the right hand of God and is also interceding for us."** Jesus is interceding for you right now. Jesus, who knows all your worst actions and thoughts, has forgiven you, and his blood poured out on your behalf has brought you into a relationship with

Him. He is waiting for you to partner with him to speak the words of love and adoration he is speaking over you, night and day. Will you join him?

Scripture shares so much insight into how deeply we are loved, and Song of Songs is a great resource to hear the heart of God and the true words of love that are constantly spoken over you. Many people have read Song of Songs and felt conflicted and confused, myself included. I recently began to read Song of Songs in The Passion Translation Bible, which includes extensive footnotes that explain the Aramaic, Greek, and Hebrew along with cultural contexts that help us to understand that the Bible beautifully describes the intimate relationship between Jesus and his Bride- The Church.

I highly recommend reading it through this lens and seeing just HOW MUCH Jesus loves you. The Bible is an incredible source of our true identity. There is nothing like reading words that God himself breathed. I encourage you to meditate on the following verses, write them out, read them out loud, and place them in prominent places around you, like your mirror, car, fridge, etc.

-Psalm 139:13-14 AMP "For You formed my innermost parts; You knit me [together] in my mother's womb. I will give thanks and praise to You, for I am fearfully and wonderfully made; Wonderful are Your works, And my soul knows it very well."

-Ephesians 2:10 AMP "For we are His workmanship [His own master work, a work of art], created in Christ Jesus [reborn from above—spiritually transformed, renewed, ready to be used] for good works, which God prepared [for us] beforehand [taking paths which He set], so that we would walk in them [living the good life which He prearranged and made ready for us]."

-1 Peter 2:9 AMP "But you are a chosen race, a royal priesthood, a consecrated nation, a [special] people for God's own possession, so that you may proclaim the excellencies [the wonderful deeds and virtues and perfections] of Him who called you out of darkness into His marvelous light."

-Zephaniah 3:17 AMP "The Lord your God is in your midst, A Warrior who saves. He will rejoice over you with joy; He will be quiet in His love [making no mention of your past sins], He will rejoice over you with shouts of joy."

The Lie: "Love is All You Need"

The lie that the love of another is enough to fulfill and heal us is so pervasive in our culture. From movies to books and songs, we are taught from a young age that there is love out there waiting for us that will make us whole. The world finds a prince charming, but the Bible teaches us it is King Jesus who comes to save, heal, love, and cherish. He is the one who will fulfill your every need and longing. He is the one who heals every wound. Will you let Him?

The Lie Breaker

Pray aloud with me:

"Holy Spirit, thank you for revealing these areas where I have allowed deception to rule in my heart and mind. I repent for allowing other loves to fill your position in my heart. I reject and walk away from any lies I have believed or spoken over myself and ask that you remove their effects on me. I ask that you fill me with your Spirit and flood me with truth where lies have dwelled. Would you fill my body, soul, and spirit with your love? I ask, Father, that you show me how you love me and fill me with the ability to receive that love. I choose to receive the freedom of the cross and love myself as you love me."

Lie #6
"I'm Not Enough."

I did not feel like I was "enough" in any area for much of my life.
I did not think I was skinny enough.
I did not think I was pretty enough.
I did not think I was smart enough.
I did not think I was loveable enough.
I did not think I was talented enough.
The list could go on for days.
"Comparison is the thief of joy" could be the quote that sums up many, many years of my life. Although I have been a professional photographer for nearly 20 years, there are many times when I have struggled even to call myself one. Comparing myself to photographers who shoot magazine-worthy images, with accolades longer than this book, caused me to be so short-sighted in the giftings God

has given me, and to be honest, often hindered me from being creative and allowing him to flow through me while shooting. I made more mistakes, thinking I would make them. I have learned that when I let go and ask God to work through me, my photographs are so much better! Striving to be perfect has led to many more imperfect moments than perfect ones. It also caused me to be incredibly self-focused and STRESSED OUT! The fear of making mistakes and not being good enough at something I was being paid to do led me to often freak out about minor shifts or things going wrong. It is tough to see The One who created us when we stay focused on ourselves. He wants us to call upon him in our weakness, to tell him we need him. He loves coming to our aid and making wrong things right for us.

What is enough? What exactly does it mean to be enough anyway? The dictionary defines enough as 'as much or as many of something as required.' To be as much of something as required. What? That is one of the most vague descriptions ever. How did we accept that we are not enough when enough doesn't know it is enough? Where does this idea of "being enough" come from? In **John 15:5 TPT**, Jesus says, **"I am the sprouting vine and you're my branches. As you live in union with me as your source, fruitfulness will stream from within you—but when you live separated from me you are powerless."** When we try to be enough, we typically are trying to do something on our own, away from the source of all of our power and strength, which is the Holy Spirit living through us.

> "But he answered me, "My grace is always more than enough for you, and my power finds its full expression through your weakness." So I will celebrate my weaknesses, for when I'm weak I sense more deeply the mighty power of Christ living in me." 2 Corinthians 12:9 TPT

Our weakness is an opportunity for Christ to be enough in us. When we cannot be enough, He can. When we fail or have flaws and needs, it is an opportunity for Him to show His glory. Knowing this literally takes the weight off, doesn't it?? What a freeing notion that I do not have to have it all together; I don't have to be perfect. **Perfection does not bring freedom, and being "enough" is a facade.**

The cross is the only way to experience total Freedom. God's ransom, which paid for my debt, brings me complete freedom and into a life of marvelous grace where I can make mistakes, throw away the idol of perfection, and run into the arms of my loving Father. He knows me by name, and He sees my heart. He knows I have made the same mistakes repeatedly, yet He loves me. He knows my heart and sees that even in ignorance, stubbornness, pride, and shame, I was turning my heart towards Him, praying that He would reach out to me, and He did. **He's doing the same for you right now.**

Maybe you had a family that required you to be good, perfect, and always be enough for everyone. Perhaps you've never heard that God could love and accept you right where you are. Maybe you've never known a love that produces more than enough. I want to extend to you the invitation to drop the heavy burdens and run into the loving arms of your Father. In Luke 15, we read the story of the prodigal son, who, after leaving his father's house with his inheritance, squandered the money and ended up living in a pig pen, eating slop. He realized that even his father's servants ate better than he did, and he decided to go home. As he was walking home, his father saw him from a far-off distance and ran to meet him and kissed him. The son dropped to his father's feet in repentance, begging to be allowed back to become a servant. The father quickly told his servants to kill the fattened calf and to prepare a banquet for his wayward son.

> "WHAT A FREEING NOTION THAT I DO NOT HAVE TO HAVE IT ALL TOGETHER; I DON'T HAVE TO BE PERFECT. PERFECTION DOES NOT BRING FREEDOM, AND BEING ENOUGH IS A FACADE."

He told them to get his rings, robes, and shoes, dress him, and celebrate his return. Jesus told this story to explain to those listening, and to you right now, sweet reader, that he CELEBRATES your run to him. You don't have to be "enough"; you just have to receive His love. The lie that you need to be enough turns the most tender heart into a broken one because it is impossible to live up to. There is no way you can ever measure up, and thank God he doesn't expect you to. His heart desires that you would prosper as your soul prospers, and your soul will prosper through intimacy with Him and by your mind being renewed.

Perfection Kills Promise

Have you ever noted God's promises regarding you that are laid out in his Word? There are many, but I want to share a few with you here:

- **He has redeemed you.** You cannot redeem yourself from the sinful nature you are born into. All of your righteous acts are considered "filthy rags" in comparison to the righteousness of Christ. When you accept His life for yours, you benefit from being made righteous, as He has redeemed you from all darkness. **"For he has rescued us from the dominion of darkness and brought us into the kingdom of the Son he loves, in whom we have redemption, the forgiveness of sins."** Colossians 1:13-14 NIV
- **He set set you free.** As an adopted heir of God, you are made free. **"So if the Son makes you free, then you are unquestionably free."** John 8:36 AMP
- **He will give you the desires of your heart.** As you walk in life with Christ, He will place an awareness of His perfect will in you and lead you toward the desires that line up with His heart. **"Delight yourself in the Lord, And He will give you the desires and petitions of your heart."** Psalm 37:4 AMP
- **He will never leave you.** God promises never to leave or forsake you. He will always keep you in the palm of His hand and won't release His hold on you. **"I will never [under any circumstances] desert you [nor give you up nor leave you without support, nor will I in any degree leave you helpless], nor will I forsake or let you down or relax my hold on you [assuredly not]!"** Hebrews 13:5 AMP

- **His love never fails.** God's love goes beyond the comprehension of human love. It is perfect and never fails. **"For the mountains may be removed and the hills may shake, but My lovingkindness will not be removed from you, nor will My covenant of peace be shaken," says the Lord who has compassion on you."** Isaiah 54:10 AMP

There are so many other promises in the Word, and they never fail concerning you and God's astounding love for you. These promises are not based on your perfection, as Ephesians explains:

> **"For by grace you have been saved by faith. Nothing you did could ever earn this salvation, for it was the love gift from God that brought us to Christ! So no one will ever be able to boast, for salvation is never a reward for good works or human striving."** Ephesians 2:8-9 TPT

You can do nothing to earn God's salvation gift, yet how many of us have struggled to feel confident in our salvation? As I shared earlier, I went to the altar for salvation many times as a kid. The pastor's sermons made me fearful because I thought of how I had disobeyed my parents or fought with my little brothers. Those fears kept me striving for perfection for years. I often felt that God was insatiable in His expectations of my perfection. As the oldest child, I was also taught that it was my job to 'set a good example' for my younger siblings and to be 'good.' I internalized the belief that perfection would keep me in the promise of salvation. Add that to the idea that I needed to look perfect and was a walking lie, ready to fail. All of God's promises were 'killed' by the striving for perfection. I was not in 'perfect peace' because my mind was not kept on God but on my looks and behavior. I did not believe in the promise of salvation because I fixated on my failures. As I grew, I did not think I would receive the desire of my heart- a husband- because I believed I was not pretty or skinny enough. I was constantly 'killing' the promise with my words and establishing a firm foundation of fear, anxiety, and confusion. I often heard sermons that taught these promises and felt they must be for someone else, someone who 'had it all together' or naturally thin, athletic, and more intelligent than me. It seemed the 'ideal' was far from who I was.

Ideals Vs. Idols

I remember getting some teen magazines in middle school and my dad telling me he didn't want me to read them. I couldn't understand why. They seemed harmless to me. I loved the fun, bright layout, with the love quizzes and new hair tutorials. The reality was that those magazines were creating a specific narrative. A narrative drenched in the beliefs that to be thin is to be beautiful, to be bigger is to be, well, less desirable. They taught that you needed to be slim, dress a certain way, style your hair a certain way, and have a persona that matched the other girls that aligned with this facade. I will never forget this one outfit I just had to have from Wet Seal. Does anybody remember Wet Seal? ● It was TURQUOISE, corduroy bell bottoms with a fuzzy (think fuzzy sock material) lime green and turquoise sweater and a SILVER pleather jacket...I looked like a character from Monsters Inc., y'all! I was so desperate to get the "look" and "fit in," but I looked hilarious. My mom, a fashionista, tried to guide me in making a different purchase, but I did not listen. What 13-year-old does? I wore that outfit to youth group one Wednesday night with my clear smiley face purse, and I thought I had arrived! However, when I got to church, I looked around the room and noticed everyone was skinnier than me, wearing Abercrombie jeans and white babydoll Ts, and I looked like a little lost highlighter. I wanted to melt into the pew. I can still remember my hands in my lap, looking down at those bright pants and feeling invisible and WAY too seen all at once. I recently talked with my mom about that outfit, and she said, "I wondered why you were obsessed with getting that outfit and then you would never wear it again."

I had created an ideal in my mind that this outfit would help me attain status and approval. I thought that I would look 'perfect' finally. Realizing I was wrong led me down a path of self-destructive thinking and depression. Not only did I not have the right outfit, but I was also heavier and taller than most of the other girls in my youth group. I am the tallest woman in my family and always felt like a giant, out of place, and awkward. Now, married to my 6'11 husband, I feel short! Funny how God works all things out, huh? I was embarrassed by my weight, even though, looking back, I was a healthy weight. But, being naturally curvier, I felt I did not align with the ideal, and therefore, I believed I was not enough. Through all of this, I made the ideal an idol.

Idols are not just statues of gods but high things, beliefs, ideas, and wants that we exalt above God Himself. My fear of not being enough led to a desperation to be 'enough,' which led me back to never feeling enough. This cycle went on for many years and brought with it great heartache. Looking back, I see all the time I wasted, not feeling like I measured up, and how much life I missed out on because of that lie. If I could say anything to the one who thinks they are not enough, I would tell them that you can never be 'enough' without intimately knowing the One who is.

Jesus is enough, and in Him, you are complete. Through him, you can have life and life more abundantly. You will never be enough in how you look, who you marry, your career, motherhood, friendship, or anything else, not in your own strength. None of those things can complete you, and they cannot deplete your value. However, the power of Jesus, living through you through the empowerment of the Holy Spirit, will enable you to do all things through Christ, who gives you strength. He is your value source. He is your identity.
Identifying Your Value

The census record that comes around every ten years and counts every citizen in the US asks a LOT of questions about who you are. It goes into fine detail regarding your ethnicity, gender, marital status, etc. It intends to capture all your details to inform the government of your identity for different research purposes. We often face identifying questions to inform people of our identity- for legal purposes, jobs, buying a house, or going to the doctor. People want to know who you are.

Do you know who you are beyond your name, title, marriage license, job, and zip code? Much of our culture in America centers around who we are as individuals. From a young age, we learn that independence is the ideal and that we are responsible for ourselves. We hear, "You can do anything you put your mind to," and you "live in the land of opportunities." All you have to do is "pull yourself up by the bootstraps." These ideals focus on you being the goal- your success, career, and needs. The problem with this view is that you are the focus when failure or setbacks occur, which is inevitable. So, what do you believe about yourself and your identity if your business fails, if you don't finish your degree, if you never marry, if you don't have kids? Who are you if the "success" doesn't happen?

In Psalms, David cries out to God, saying,

"You saw who you created me to be before I became me! Before I'd ever seen the light of day, the number of days you planned for me were already recorded in your book. Every single moment you are thinking of me! How precious and wonderful to consider that you cherish me constantly in your every thought! O God, your desires toward me are more than the grains of sand on every shore! When I awake each morning, you're still with me." Psalm 139:16-18 TPT.

Before you ever chose a career or felt 'called', God saw who He created you to be: His child. As His child, you receive the FULL inheritance that Jesus died to restore for you. "**Through our union with Christ we too have been claimed by God as his own inheritance. Before we were even born, he gave us our destiny, that we would fulfill the plan of God who always accomplishes every purpose and plan in his heart.**" **Ephesians 1:11 TPT**. God gave us a destiny to fulfill, but He first gave us an identity. We are His heirs. When we become reborn, we die to our old selves and rise with Christ, "**We are reborn into a perfect inheritance that can never perish, never be defiled, and never diminish. It is promised and preserved forever in the heavenly realm for you!**" 1 Peter 1:4 TPT

Paul shares, "**Every spiritual blessing in the heavenly realm has already been lavished upon us as a love gift from our wonderful heavenly Father, the Father of our Lord Jesus—all because he sees us wrapped in Christ. This is why we celebrate him with all our hearts!**" **Ephesians 1:3 TPT.** We do not have to seek approval from anyone, and we never have to find a title to receive value. We are approved and valuable simply because we are children of God.

The Lie: "I am Not Enough."

From the perspective of the world, we will never be enough. Our culture and industry push us to want to continue buying all the new clothes, new makeup, new supplements, new skincare, etc. Every ad seeks to reach those who have a 'need.' This doesn't mean you shouldn't buy new items; just start recognizing that in Christ, you are enough. Is your beauty and significance firmly planted in that truth? If not, why? What lies have you believed that have kept you from that truth?

The Lie Breaker

Pray aloud with me:

"In the name of Jesus Christ, I sever the lie that I am not enough. Through Jesus Christ, I am made holy, acceptable, and sufficient by His will and strength. I repent for agreeing with the lie that I can and should be perfect. I repent for trying to control my life. I release myself from my judgment. I receive the truth that I am the righteousness of God in Christ Jesus and that by His blood I have been redeemed and walk in His authority. I receive my identity from God alone. I receive my value from the cross. Thank you, Jesus, for dying for me, living in me, and bringing me into true freedom. Amen."

Lie #7

"God is Not Enough."

For most of my life, I assumed idols were just little statues of false gods, like little Buddhas in restaurants. I had no idea that an idol could be a mindset, a belief, or even a person. An idol is anything we make higher, more important, more valued than God. When we reach for things, people, and ideas that we believe can rescue us or provide us with all we are missing, we tell God that He is not enough. Some of our idols are obvious and might even be spotted by those in our lives. Others are a bit more concealed. It is challenging to realize the idols that we have in our minds because they are often attached to justified thoughts. For example, I love my husband; I desire to care for him, cherish him, and be the best wife I can be for him. I think about him throughout the day, and he's typically the first person I speak to daily and the last at night. We spend many hours together a week. We catch up throughout the day and call each other when we're apart. There is nothing wrong with the time I spend with him or the thoughts I have about him unless those times keep me away from God or unless those thoughts turn into ungodly beliefs. If I start believing that I am not valuable unless I am a wife, that being married completes me, or that my husband is my everything, I have made marriage and my husband an idol. Anything that sits in God's place in our hearts can become an idol. We must take inventory of where our hearts are and what we focus on to ensure our life's foundation is not set on an idol but on Christ alone.

I believe we often slip into idolization because we have experienced feeling like we are not enough, feeling like bad things have happened to us, or because we feel that God has not moved in our situation in the way we wanted. We grab ahold of things that feel as though they can save, empower, or assist us when, in fact, those "things" are often the things that will drag us down or keep us in bondage to them. We may not even realize it, but we begin to feel that the little idols we can see are better than a God we can't.

The Idol of Image

Idols are cheap imitations of the real thing. They are flimsy and fail. Idols require a sacrifice and cause crippling limitations. Adoration of an idol, given through time, thoughts, and actions, will increase its ability to stand in your life. The lie that you are not enough and that you would be happier if you were skinnier is increased by reality TV, social media, books, movies, songs, and a culture that values looks and sex appeal over the heart.

I certainly made my image an idol in the past. I thought about my weight **constantly**. My entire life hinged around how I looked, what I would wear, how I might have to act or what I would have to do in specific environments and how I might look doing those things- like having to walk down an aisle at a wedding, or jog across the gym at school, or anything that would allow people to see me. My thoughts were bound to the way I looked, and they kept me in what felt like a prison cell. I could not tap into the truth of who God said I was. I had barricaded myself behind a wall that I was a failure. That wall built up day after day as thoughts came over and over like a brick after brick. The demonic lies I heard became strongholds in my mind, and I glued those bricks together with my words, speaking negatively over myself all day long. **"For where your treasure is, there your heart will be also." Luke 12:34 AMP**
I treasured being skinny and how I looked; that was where my heart was found.

Throughout the Bible, we see individuals who placed a value, which could be an idol, on things other than God and how devastating the results were. Solomon, the wisest man in the Bible, had the ear of God and was filled with the knowledge of God, placed value on women, and they became his downfall. **"As Solomon grew old, his wives turned his heart after other gods, and his heart was not fully devoted to the LORD his God, as the heart of David his father had been." 1 Kings 11:4 NIV**

He married women from other countries with false gods, and he began to drift away from the true God whom he had known so intimately, leading to his kingdom's demise.

While Moses was up on the mountain for 40 days communing with God, the people down below turned against God, saying to Moses' brother Aaron, **"Come, make us a god who will go before us; as for this Moses, the man who brought us up from the land of Egypt, we do not know what has become of him."** Exodus 32:1 **NASB.** It is important to note that the people said "the man who brought us out of Egypt"- they had just been set free from slavery by the power of God through Moses, yet they doubted that he would return, and they required a god to be made in his absence. In chapter 19, they experienced the awe of God coming with His presence to Mount Sinai, yet they had forgotten. They could not see the real thing among them and wanted a false thing they could touch and see. So, Aaron had all of the people come together, bringing their golden jewelry, and made a golden calf, and the people began to make sacrifices to it and worship it as if it was the Lord that brought them out of Egypt.

We can quickly start idolizing anything. When we begin to idolize our physical appearance, weight, and more, we may soon feel inadequate because the idol is always "perfect" by society's standards, and we cannot measure up to perfect. As I discussed earlier in the book, supermodels have long been the beauty standard, and these women are typically the "perfect" size. The photos of these women, with no hair out of place, perfect makeup, clothes, and lighting create a fake image that no one can compete with. The whole image is a farce, likely crafted in Photoshop. It is impossible to measure up to something that isn't even real! No one walks around with that perfect environment to maintain their looks, and to be honest, who would want to? How exhausting would that be? Beyond that, to think our weight brings value is a very shallow existence, isn't it?

The idea that our size and image will bring us worth and value shows how desperately we need to be truly validated by the one who loves our souls. We need the love of Jesus to permeate our thoughts. We must repent and ask Him to tear down every idol we have placed in his way. To idolize our size and image daily by setting it as a priority in our thoughts is to miss our freedom bought on the cross altogether.

> "THE IDEA THAT OUR SIZE AND IMAGE WILL BRING US WORTH AND VALUE SHOWS HOW DESPERATELY WE NEED TO BE TRULY VALIDATED BY THE ONE WHO LOVES OUR SOULS."

There was a day when I realized that I had been idolizing my weight, and all of a sudden, it was as if the Lord Himself came into the room and told me that I was making my weight and my looks more important than Him. I felt terrible! I grieved that I had allowed vanity in the place of the one who saved me. I quickly began to repent, asking Him to forgive me and turn me from this thinking. I cried and cried as I prayed, releasing not only my disappointment in my actions but much of the disdain I held for myself. As I cried, He was healing many of the stored-up painful memories I had about myself. Releasing forgiveness for myself and all those who have hurt me was one of the most significant pieces of this journey. Forgiveness is one of the most essential parts of this book, and there will be more discussion surrounding forgiveness in a later chapter.

The Idol of Status

Growing up, I often daydreamed about what my future would look like. My friends and I would play house, pretending to be a mom, carrying around baby dolls, making "soup," and flipping plastic eggs in our little kitchens. We would pretend to go to work, carrying our purses and wearing our mom's old high heels, imagining the glamour we were heading into for the day. As I grew, I never had a specific dream of something I wanted to "be" when I grew up. I had no aspirations of fame, fortune, or career. I looked up to my mom, a fantastic wife and homemaker, and assumed I would follow in her footsteps. In high school, I spent three years in a program called Pro-Start, which assisted students in being professionally trained in careers. I learned from chefs about the culinary arts, front and back-of-the-house management for restaurants and hotels. I toured many establishments, such as the Ritz Carleton, The Cheesecake Factory, and Barnsley Gardens, learning how great culinary and hospitality industries run. I had been accepted to culinary school and planned to become a chef. After my dad passed away my Junior year of high school, I began to shift my career focus. I felt lost and unsure of what I should do.

In the spring of my senior year, I begrudgingly toured Lee University after a friend's insistence. When I arrived, and my foot touched the campus ground, I felt God's presence, and there was a sweeping peace in my soul telling me that this was where I was supposed to be. All other plans shifted, and I began my studies at Lee that Fall. Although I felt confident about where to attend school, I still needed to figure out what to do.

Many people find their worth, value, and status in their careers, money, fame, etc. I believed I would receive my worth and status through marriage. I shared earlier that I thought that a man would help me to love myself, that I would be 'healed' and become 'whole' in the right relationship, but I also believed that I would have status because I would be a wife. And I wasn't the only one who held this idea. There was no more significant title in the vocabulary of an early 2000s young woman at Lee University.

On my first day on campus, I saw a huge banner on one of the buildings that said, "Come get your M.R.S. Degree Here!" In my mind, I could not be anything until I became a wife. I felt unsure of how to choose a major, honestly thinking, what if I meet my husband and my major competes with his, or if it doesn't complement him, or what if he won't like what I do for work? The strangest thoughts would go through my mind, all surrounding this fictional husband. I felt as if I did not exist because I was not married.

Growing up during the height of "purity culture," I attended the I Kissed Dating Goodbye conference and heard all about saving yourself for your husband. While remaining pure is holy and good, the hyper-fixation of becoming a wife and attuning your whole life to preparing to become one was unhealthy. At church and among my family, I learned the belief that I was made to be a wife and mother. I was never told I could have a career or purpose outside of being a wife and mother. I say this all the time, especially to my single friends: **Marriage is not the crown of life. Marriage is good, holy, and beautiful, but it is not the goal of our lives; living for Jesus and loving others is the goal.**

When I started dating a guy in college, we talked a lot about marriage. We were raised to be abstinent and to date with the intention of marriage. Our major talks revolved around what we wanted from our spouse, what marriage to the other would look like, and how we needed to shift to make that happen. Even though we were only friends for an extended period, I often made decisions based on his needs, schedule, job, etc. I felt connected to him and as if my purpose had increased because he was in my life. We talked a lot about doing ministry together, how our calling, degrees, and careers lined up, and we spent a lot of time with each other's families. I was so pleased to be called his girlfriend as if the added title had given me more worth. We spent three years dating off and on, with large "breaks" sprinkled throughout. Whenever we were on a break, I would find myself feeling untethered, unsure of what to do with my life. It felt like the break could make or break me.

In the late Summer of 2008, we were on one of these breaks. We were deciding whether to proceed towards engagement or break up for good. We had agreed upon three days apart to pray and separate from one another without communication. I'll never forget, late one August night, I received an impression from God to "Go and end it. Forever." I drove to his house and asked him to meet me outside. I told him that we were done, forever. We were never getting back together. (Taylor Swift owes me some money because I said it first!) He said, "Ok." and that was it. Strangely enough, I felt liberated. I went home that night and cut my hair myself, hacking off about 8 inches in the bathroom of my apartment. I believe the Lord was beginning to take me on a journey of breaking me of the lie that I needed a guy to have status and worth.

Not long after that, my now husband reached out to me and asked how I was doing. I told him I was good but wanted to get out of the house to do something fun. We ended up hanging out a few weeks later, and the rest is history! While I had started hearing from the Lord about my worth and that my position was not contingent on my relationship status, I still deeply desired to be a wife.

My husband and I fell in love quickly and were engaged a little over a year after our first date. As I mentioned, my husband Desmond is 6'11 and draws much attention wherever he goes. He played professional basketball, was inundated with fans, and has always been esteemed by others. I was madly in love with Des, and getting engaged to a basketball player at our small Christian college made me feel like a princess. I was asked to walk the court with him on Senior Night and genuinely felt like I had finally arrived. I couldn't care less about my psychology degree or future career. I just wanted to be Mrs. Desmond Blue. I idolized that title. Selecting the status of engaged on my Facebook profile brought me to tears. Being a fiancée made me feel as if my status in the world had increased. As I shared, I grew up believing that becoming a wife was the most incredible honor by well-meaning family and friends, but it was an idol in my life, and I could not see that then. As I entered our marriage, I believed I was finally becoming what I was supposed to be.

When my name changed to Jill Blue on Facebook and my status to wife, I was the happiest girl in the world, yet the high did not last. The realities of married life amid a major recession hit hard and fast. We struggled not just paycheck to paycheck but day to day. We could not find work anywhere, and suddenly, we were struggling to get food on the table. Marriage quickly went from a fun identifier to a stress-filled reality. My identity had been so wrapped up in getting married that I did not know who I was. I was a wife without understanding what that meant, especially as I did not know who I was.

God never desires for us to idolize the things He's given us over Him, the giver. When we begin to idolize things, He will often shift them to place our focus back onto Him. Our marriage went through several tough years, and the idol of being a wife came crashing down. God used those challenging times to reveal to me that marriage meant sacrifice, giving of yourself, and not just getting the ideal title of wife. God started to challenge my misguided belief that marriage would fulfill my calling in life as He began to teach me that I was created and called to worship Him alone. I was made and called to live my life for God. He taught me marriage is more about honoring God than receiving a dream life or title.

I have realized that to be happily married means to be obedient to God, even when it is painful or uncomfortable. He has used my position as a wife to sharpen, refine, and teach me how to be the daughter he always created me to be. He has used my husband in my life as a mirror to see my heart's true nature, hold me accountable, and call me higher.

Marriage is one of the most refining processes you can go through. I think that is why the divorce rate is so high. We don't like to see the worst parts of ourselves, let alone have someone else hold us accountable for our actions during those worst moments. Desmond has been such a fantastic help to me. He sees when I am tired and emotionally worn down, and when my flesh begins to flare, he will stop and start praying for me, knowing that prayer is the best course of action. I thank God for my marriage and pray daily for Desmond. I pray that our marriage makes us more like Jesus and that we can accomplish greater for His kingdom together.

You are so valuable, whether married or single. No person on this earth can love and satisfy you like Jesus. If you have placed marriage on a pedestal, I invite you to ask Holy Spirit to tear it down to show you who you are. If your marriage has been an idol, I invite you to let God in to reveal that to you and ask Him to purge you of every idol and replace it with His truth and love.

The Idol of Motherhood

In the Bible, we see how Sarah put her value in being a mother. She felt as though she was not enough because she could not conceive a child. This led to her rushing ahead of God's plan. She gave her servant to her husband so that she could provide a son for Abraham in her place. This decision led to such devastation for Sarah, her servant Haggar, Haggar's son Ishmael, and many descendants that have followed since.

As God has challenged me to release the idol of my status being attached to anything but Him, I have realized the other ways I have put things in His place. As I shared, I always wanted to be a wife and a mother. Desmond and I stopped preventing pregnancy about two years after we got married. In the Fall of 2012, I had a positive pregnancy test and a negative blood test. The nurse called it a 'chemical pregnancy,' and I thought that meant it was an accidental reading. I felt a lot of grief for years and was not sure why. It was not until a few years ago that I learned that a 'chemical pregnancy' is just a term used for a very early miscarriage.

Desmond and I continued not to prevent pregnancy after that, and months became years, and years have become over a decade of trying for children. Around 2016, at my highest weight, I was also at my lowest place. The desire to be a mother was a huge idol in my life. I built my life around the desire to get pregnant. Depression wove around my heart like a weighted blanket, and I started relying on other things to soothe my aching heart. I was addicted to sugar, as I shared, and I ate my feelings all the time. I also began to smoke weed at night to try to get to sleep. That time in my life feels like a whirlwind of sadness. It was a time when I struggled to find any purpose in my life.

One night, the Lord spoke to my heart and told me he made me for more than this. He told me that I needed to fill my life with things that did not steal Life from it. I stopped smoking weed, and that Fall, I surrendered my life and the food addiction to Him. I believe the Lord used that very dark season in my life to bring me to a place of total dependency on Him. He took every idol I had erected above Him and took them down, piece by piece. He will not tolerate other gods before him, but in His mighty love, He comes and tears down these idols and builds up our most holy faith in their place. In His love, He comes and shows us that He is SO much better than we could ever imagine. He shows up and proves that no other thing can compare to His goodness and faithfulness. All idols have to bow to Him.

"We know that anyone born of God does not continue to sin; the One who was born of God keeps them safe, and the evil one cannot harm them. We know that we are children of God, and that the whole world is under the control of the evil one. We know also that the Son of God has come and has given us understanding, so that we may know him who is true. And we are in him who is true by being in his Son Jesus Christ. He is the true God and eternal life. Dear children, keep yourselves from idols." 1 John 5:18-21

The Lie: "God is Not Enough."

God is incredibly faithful, and He is not angry with you if you have stepped into believing that He is not enough. He desires that you repent for idolatry, turn away from faulty thinking, and be restored to the truth that He is good and true, and can always repair any broken place in your life. He loves you deeply.

The Lie Breaker

I invite you to pray aloud:

"Holy Spirit, I invite you to reveal all the ways I have believed you are not enough. Please show me what I have allowed to become idols in my life. I repent for making _____ (state your idols) an idol and for allowing it/them to become more important than you. I repent for not trusting you with my whole heart. I ask that you would tear down and remove everything that has been exalted above you and that in their place, you would sit, enthroned in my heart. I choose to trust you. I choose to relinquish control and repent for trying to control my own life. I need you, I love you, and I give you permission to have your way. Would you come, Holy Spirit, and fill me, and change everything?"

Lie #8
"I'll Never Be Free."

For many years I believed the lie that I always felt, that I would never be free. It felt like everyone I knew was progressing in their lives, moving forward with their calling, career, and relationships, and I felt stuck. In my mind, it seemed I would never be able to progress. I often felt unsure of why I was put on the earth. While reading through some of my journals from 2004, I cried out to God, telling Him, **"God, I feel like you are forgetting about me! I am hurting inside, and I feel so lost."** That page is covered in tear stains as I cried out to God, feeling that He was far from me. Several pages later, I wrote, **"Lord, at times, I feel like I am so lost. I can't see your plan for me anywhere."** I constantly felt as if I was adrift, unsure of my purpose. The only constant thing was the voice I heard hispering, saying, "He doesn't hear you, He doesn't care. You still feel the same way, day after day. It will never change." My ears were opened to the voices of evil, and I could not escape their lies. I experienced torment in my body, soul, and spirit, and I suffered for many years and had no idea how to stop it.

"Now, may the God of peace and harmony set you apart, making you completely holy. And may your entire being—spirit, soul, and body—be kept completely flawless in the appearing of our Lord Jesus, the Anointed One. The one who calls you by name is trustworthy and will thoroughly complete his work in you." Thessalonians 5:23-24 TPT

Spirit, Soul & Body

The God of peace is currently sanctifying us, body, soul, and spirit. Torrace Solomon states, "Jesus will come and find the parts of you that are not in agreement with Him." Learning the following information has really helped me to make sense of the experiences I have had and has given imagery to what I have learned. We are made up of three parts: we are a spirit that is eternal, that has a soul, which makes up our mind, will, and emotions, which creates our unique personality, and that is all housed in a mortal body.

Spirit *eternal*
⇐
- Gifts of the spirit
- Supernatural senses
- Faith

Soul *eternal*
⇐
- Mind
- Desire
- Will
- Reason
- Personality
- Emotion
- Fruit of the Spirit
- Thought

Body *temporary*
⇐
- Systems
- Health
- Senses
- Organs
- Physical shell

The Spirit

Your spirit was born in the mind of God and placed in your mother's womb and cannot be owned by anyone but God. He created you through His **ruach**- the Hebrew word for breath- and therefore, you are His, regardless of your behavior. He has total and forever ownership over your spirit. The Bible explains, **"Surely I was sinful at birth, sinful from the time my mother conceived me." Psalm 51:5 NIV.**

This is why you don't have to teach a child to sin, they inherently know how to. We were born dead, spiritually. Your spirit is eternal and will always exist, either in the presence of God for eternity or apart from His presence for eternity. When we receive Jesus as our Lord, we become ALIVE for the first time, therefore, 'Born Again.' Living a life submitted to Christ as our Lord means we will be with him in eternity. Your spirit is redeemed when you are born again, always to be clothed in garments of righteousness. Your spirit will never be taken from the presence of God after you are submitted to Jesus.

"YOUR SPIRIT WAS BORN IN THE MIND OF GOD AND PLACED IN YOUR MOTHER'S WOMB AND CANNOT BE OWNED BY ANYONE BUT GOD."

The Soul

The soul houses our Mind, Will, and Emotions, which all go through the processes of sanctification or being purified or made holy. **"The spirit (conscience) of man is the lamp of the Lord, searching and examining all the innermost parts of his being." Proverbs 20:27 AMP.** The spirit listed here is the Hebrew word **nᵉshâmâh,** which means wind or breath and is used to describe the Spirit of God, the spirit of man, and every breathing thing. The innermost part (belly) is the Hebrew word **beṭenan** again, which means soul. The Spirit of God is a lamp searching the soul of man to find places that do not line up with Him and to expose the darkness, bringing light and truth. This reveals that even those who have come into His marvelous light and are now the children of God are still being sanctified in their souls, where there are still places of darkness. Torrace Solomon explains, "You only need light when there is darkness. When you get saved your spirit is regenerated, but your soul doesn't. Your spirit and your flesh are at war with one another-this is why you often feel divided."

The Body

Our bodies house our spirit and soul. They are ever-changing and will eventually perish. We were created to glorify God and to bring him honor. **"We know that our old self [our human nature without the Holy Spirit] was nailed to the cross with Him, in order that our body of sin might be done away with, so that we would no longer be slaves to sin. For the person who has died [with Christ] has been freed from [the power of] sin." Romans 6:6-7 AMP.**

As we die with Christ and rise with him, our bodies, while dying, house our spirit, that will live forever. Having a body allows us to fulfill the scripture that we are called to **"Heal the sick, raise the dead, cleanse the lepers, cast out demons..." Matthew 10:8 AMP.** We continue his work on earth as we submit to Jesus and give Him permission to live through us.

> "I assure you and most solemnly say to you, anyone who believes in Me [as Savior] will also do the things that I do; and he will do even greater things than these [in extent and outreach], because I am going to the Father. 13 And I will do whatever you ask in My name [[b]as My representative], this I will do, so that the Father may be glorified and celebrated in the Son. 14 If you ask Me anything in My name [as My representative], I will do it." John 14:12-14 AMP

How often do we align with some form of the world's phrase that it's "our body"? We believe that we should have total autonomy over our body and that we get to make the decisions for and about it. 1 Corinthians 6:19 tells us that the Holy Spirit calls our bodies His temple, His sanctuary and that they are a gift, not our property. He has given us our bodies on loan as a gift for his earthly purposes. It is so important that we talk with Holy Spirit about our bodies and include Him in our decisions regarding it. We are to glorify God with every action we take, not use our bodies for our pleasure. When our actions go against God's desires for us, and when they dishonor him, we abuse the gift.

Becoming Free Indeed

I have mentioned several times throughout this book that I have been set free indeed from a spirit of heaviness, a spirit of rejection, and I want to give a bit more information on what I mean by that. For most of my life I had heard about the devil and demons, but I had no idea how they might literally be impacting my daily life, all the while they were impacting my life every day. These tormenting thoughts and whispers I heard were the influence of demonic voices that had been given access to my soul- my mind, will and emotions- through places of bitterness, unforgiveness and trauma that I had endured.

Like I said before, I did not understand the demonic realm, and I did not think Christians could "have" demons. I just thought I was mentally unstable and was on anti-depressants and anti-anxiety medications for over 10 years. I'm not saying that you should not take medications or that every bout of depression and anxiety is demonic, but for me, much of what I was feeling was rooted in demonic influence in my life. Satan's minions were always at the door of my mind, sending demonic influence to whisper lies over me. Hearing those lies sounded like my own voice, so thinking they were my own thoughts, I spoke them out over myself, giving them ground to grow within me, giving them legal right to stay.

"THE ENEMY CANNOT READ YOUR THOUGHTS, BUT HE IS STANDING AT THE DOOR OF YOUR GATES TRYING TO CONVINCE YOU TO LET HIM IN."
-TORRENCE SOLOMON

I gave permission to these evil entities to bombard me with lies because I agreed with them! I would say horrible things about myself and those demons just got more comfortable.

If you are like me for the first 35 years of my life, you are probably thinking, this doesn't make sense because verses like **2 Corinthians 6:14 AMP** says, **"...For what partnership can righteousness have with lawlessness? Or what fellowship can light have with darkness?"**. This verse however does not say that light cannot fellowship with darkness, but what fellowship can they have? John 10 gives the example of a thief that comes to steal, kill and destroy. If you leave a window open and return home to find a robber there, does he own your home now? No! However, he is IN your home and will steal, destroy and possibly kill, unless you have him arrested and kicked out!

Light and Dark

In 1 Kings 22, Isreal's King Ahab desired to fight the king of Ramoth Gilead to take back the land they inhabited. He asked the prophet Jehoshaphat if he would go with him in battle-meaning would he support the fight. Jehoshaphat told him to seek the counsel of the Lord. **"Then the king of Israel gathered the prophets together, about four hundred men, and said to them, "Shall I go to battle against Ramoth-gilead, or should I not?" And they said, "Go up, for the Lord has handed it over to the king." But Jehoshaphat [doubted and] said, "Is there not another prophet of the Lord here whom we may ask?"** 1 Kings 22:6-7 AMP. King Ahab answered that there was one other prophet but that he didn't want to hear from him because he never told Ahab what he wanted to hear. Nevertheless, Ahab brought the prophet Micaiah out of prison. The other prophets gathered around the throne, telling Ahab what he wanted to hear, but Micaiah arrived with a different prophecy. Micaiah continued,

> "Therefore hear the word of the Lord: I saw the Lord sitting on his throne with all the multitudes of heaven standing around him on his right and on his left. And the Lord said, 'Who will entice Ahab into attacking Ramoth Gilead and going to his death there?' Then a spirit came forward and stood before the Lord and said, 'I will entice him.' The Lord said to him, 'How?' And he said, 'I will go out and be a deceiving spirit in the mouth of all his prophets.' Then the Lord said, 'You are to entice him and also succeed. Go and do so.' Now then, behold, the Lord has put a deceiving spirit in the mouth of all these prophets; and the Lord has proclaimed disaster against you." 1 Kings 22:19-23

Here, we see that God is speaking with a demonic spirit, in heaven, around His throne. This example shows us that not only are demons real but that they can be in the presence of light. God himself used the demons to send disaster to Ahab.

The belief that Christians cannot be under demonic influence is often due to the misunderstanding of the word possession. In Mark 5, we read the story of the demonized man. He had been tormented by a legion of demons for many years. A legion at that time was a Roman term to describe over 5,000 soldiers. This man was under such demonic influence that he had been chained like an animal, and broken loose in the outskirts of town. As Jesus approached the man ran to him and bowed down to worship him.

> "When he saw Jesus from a distance, he ran and fell on his knees in front of him. He shouted at the top of his voice, "What do you want with me, Jesus, Son of the Most High God? In God's name don't torture me!" For Jesus had said to him, "Come out of this man, you impure spirit!" Then Jesus asked him, "What is your name?" "My name is Legion," he replied, "for we are many." And he begged Jesus again and again not to send them out of the area. A large herd of pigs was feeding on the nearby hillside. The demons begged Jesus, "Send us among the pigs; allow us to go into them." He gave them permission, and the impure spirits came out and went into the pigs. The herd, about two thousand in number, rushed down the steep bank into the lake and were drowned." Mark 5:6-13 AMP

In Greek, the phrase demon-possessed is **daimonizomai**, which means "to be under the power of a demon." In **Luke 21:19 NKJV** we read, **"By your patience possess your souls."** This word possess does not mean that God is instructing us to possess our own souls, as He is the only one who can own us. It means to gain mastery over, to obtain, or to have power over. In other words, no one but God can truly possess a person's soul. However, we can choose who has mastery over it. **People who don't believe that they can be in bondage are often those who do not experience true freedom.** If we get hung up on the semantics of a word and allow the spirit of fear to rule our hearts and minds, then we may stay in bondage for the rest of our lives. To truly be free, indeed, we must submit to the knowledge that there may be areas of our lives that we have not mastered, areas that may be under demonic influence. We must surrender all pride and allow Holy Spirit to come and bring us true freedom.

The Lie: "I'll Never be Free."

The enemy desires that you would stay in bondage for the rest of your life. He has implemented strategies that prevent you from seeing his influence in your life. He does this with every person who allows him access through many avenues, such as unforgiveness, bitterness, offense, sin cycles, trauma, and more. Today, I invite you to open your heart to the truth that through Jesus, you can be fully free.

The Lie Breaker

Would you pray aloud with me?

"Dear Jesus, Thank you for choosing me, as the joy set before you when you went to the cross. Thank you for dying for me and for making way for me to live free from all bondage and sin. I repent for taking things into my own hands. I repent for trying to live my life under my terms. I repent for not allowing you total access and control. I confess and repent for committing the sins of _____(list your sins and those known in your family line, i.e. adultery in the family.) I receive your forgiveness over myself and my family line. I thank you, Jesus, for coming and bringing me into your family line. Thank you for healing my body, soul, and spirit. Thank you for healing every wound on my soul. Would you bring me into a deeper knowledge of you and your love for me? I give you all of me. I love you. Amen."

Lie #9
"I Can't Forgive Them."

"The Holy Spirit of God has sealed you in Jesus Christ until you experience your full salvation. So never grieve the Spirit of God or take for granted his holy influence in your life. Lay aside bitter words, temper tantrums, revenge, profanity, and insults. But instead be kind and affectionate toward one another. Has God graciously forgiven you? Then graciously forgive one another in the depths of Christ's love."
Ephesians 4:30-32 TPT

Have you ever considered that some of the repetitive cycles you are stuck in could be related to unforgiveness? You may or may not have a demonic influence in your life, but I can tell you one thing: Unforgiveness gives demons the legal right to be in your life. Unforgiveness is like Miracle Grow for demonic influence in our lives. When we choose not to forgive, we partner with the enemy instead of partnering with the cross.

I often hear clients say, "I can't forgive them," referring to those who have hurt them. Whenever I hear this statement, my heart grieves. I know a terrible wrong has happened for such a statement to be said. Most people do not go around harboring unforgiveness for petty offenses. However, they often struggle to release forgiveness for major hurts, traumas, and pains they have endured. People say, "They don't deserve forgiveness," and "I don't want to forgive them." Hurts pile up, trauma takes a stand, and the wounded person gets left behind a wall of unforgiveness, feeling that the only way to survive is to block it off.

I want to tell you, dear reader, if you are standing behind the wall of unforgiveness, I see you. It is unbearably hard to release forgiveness over those who have hurt you. I know it feels like you are 'letting them off the hook' or 'telling them that what they did was ok.' The reality is that you, in your own strength, can never forgive anyone. But, through the power of the cross and the love of Jesus, you can extend His forgiveness to the ones who have harmed you. You can forgive yourself, and you can forgive God. You can be free.

Dangers of Unforgiveness

Unforgiveness is a form of pride in the life of the believer. It masks a belief that the person who has hurt, harmed, or offended you deserves less grace than you do. **James 4:6 NIV** shows us, "...**That is why Scripture says: "God opposes the proud but shows favor to the humble."**

God opposes the proud, which means he resists the proud. I don't know about you, but I do not want God to resist me. When we stay hurt and offended, we remain under pride. **"Pride keeps you from repentance, which will set you free. If you can't even admit you're offended, you cannot get free. You insist you arent offended and don't truly deal with offense and then you refuse to repent,"** which keeps you stuck in bondage.

The Root of Bitterness

Unforgiveness is a massive root of the tree of Bitterness. Bitterness is a demonic influence that comes in when someone has hurt you, and you feel you cannot forgive them. **Hebrews 12:14-17 NIV** warns, **"Make every effort to live in peace with everyone and to be holy; without holiness no one will see the Lord. See to it that no one falls short of the grace of God and that no bitter root grows up to cause trouble and defile many."** Bitterness is hard to detect as it often hides behind hurt and emotional pain. We often have so much hurt that we cannot see the bitterness because of our tears.

As a child, I received a lot of punishments. My dad took 'spare the rod, spoil the child' seriously. He was passionate about his kids being honorable, obedient Christians, and he believed it was his job to enforce teachings that would keep us in line with Biblical truth. I know he had great intentions, but I internalized a lot of lies that I was not good enough, not thin enough, not smart enough, and I walked around hurt and wounded.

Weaver, J. (2022, December 12). 12 December spirit of offense part 1. The Core Group. https://jwonlineacademy.teachable.com/courses/coregroupsignup/lectures/44532170

I would not have known bitterness was the tree because the hurt was the predominant emotion. I did not have an active desire for revenge, although I felt anger when I was younger. However, through much prayer and time with the Lord, I realized I had a bitter root toward my dad. The Lord led me into intentional prayer times, releasing my dad from my judgment and repenting for partnering with bitterness. I did not realize that there were still threads of unforgiveness attached to that bitterness. I had prayed the prayer of forgiveness over my dad so many times, and so I thought I was good to go. The Lord is faithful to reveal the inner places of our hearts if we will listen and obey.

I have a sticky note on my computer that I wrote months ago that says: 'Search my heart, Oh God. Show me any wicked way in me. Reveal any sin, unforgiveness, or hurts, and help me to repent and release them.' I look down at that note often and pray it aloud or in my heart. I know that forgiveness is the only way to live free truly. I don't want anything to tie me up in bondage. There's a saying that 'unforgiveness is like you drinking poison and waiting for the other person to die,' meaning that you are the one who truly suffers because unforgiveness breeds bitterness. Bitterness produces sickness in your spirit, soul, and body. "Studies have shown that bitter, angry people have higher blood pressure and heart rate and are more likely to die of heart disease and other illnesses." Our bodies perceive people as threats that we must fight when we feel anger and bitterness toward them. This fight mode keeps our bodies in a physiological state of dis-ease.

---

http://www.cnn.com/2011/HEALTH/08/17/bitter.resentful.ep/index.html

Difficulties in Forgiving

Andy Reese and Jennifer Barnett, authors of Freedom Tools, discuss three areas that often create difficulties in forgiving. **1. Feeling there is an unpaid debt, 2. Holding judgment against the perpetrator, and 3. Holding expectations towards the perpetrator.** They continue explaining that when people feel there is an unpaid debt, they will stay in a place of anger and keep themselves preoccupied. The person might stay grieved about the situation and have thoughts of revenge or avoidance if they see the person who hurt them. When people struggle with judgment, they will feel tired and out of sorts and may struggle with being judged by others. When the person carries around unmet expectations from the perpetrator, they may become stuck in emotionally controlling situations. They often feel stuck in relationships, unable to move on, and never feel their needs are met.

Forgiveness Brings Freedom

Releasing forgiveness over those who hurt you is one of the most important things you can do as you start the process of healing and receiving freedom. The Bible tells us, **"And when you pray, make sure you forgive the faults of others so that your Father in heaven will also forgive you. But if you withhold forgiveness from others, your Father withholds forgiveness from you." Matt 6:14-15 TPT.** While this may sound harsh, it is a necessary truth that we must learn. God has specific instructions for his people, and forgiveness is one of them. As Jesus lay nailed to the cross, he cried out to his Father, **"...Father, forgive them; for they do not know what they are doing." Luke 23:34 AMP.**

_{Reese, A. J., & Barnett, J. R. (2008). Freedom Tools (2nd ed., p. 125). Chosen Books.}

Jesus understands the weight and pain that you feel. He understands how tough it is to forgive those who have hurt you, and he says you must, but you don't have to do it alone. The power of Christ within you has given you the ability to forgive all who have hurt you, even those who don't deserve it, and will never ask for forgiveness or acknowledge how badly they hurt you.

Forgiveness is one of the keys to total freedom, and it often opens us up to all that God has in store for us. Jesus told the disciples, **"For this is the blood that seals the new covenant. It will be poured out for many for the complete forgiveness of sins."** Matthew 26:28 TPT. Jesus has already forgiven those who accept him. He bought the rights to your total freedom. It has always been God's will to bring you into complete freedom.

How to Forgive

Forgiveness sounds simple enough; pray to God and tell him I forgive so-and-so for doing blank. However, just saying the words is not enough. Forgiveness is more than words; it is an intention of the heart. Karen Swartz, M.D., said, **"Forgiveness is not just about saying the words. It is an active process in which you make a conscious decision to let go of negative feelings whether the person deserves it or not."** When we think about it, we see that we were never deserving of Jesus' forgiveness either, and yet he forgave us before the foundations of the earth were laid. He forgave us, knowing full well all of the sins we would commit, all the ones we would think, too. Forgiveness can feel very hard. It is emotionally challenging and can require a choice to submit and obey, even when you don't feel like

---
https://www.hopkinsmedicine.org/health/wellness-and-prevention/forgiveness-your-health-depends-on-it

it. Thankfully, Jesus dying on the cross made way for us not to pay the price for forgiveness; we partner with him to apply it to the situation. **"Do not judge [others self-righteously], and you will not be judged; do not condemn [others when you are guilty and unrepentant], and you will not be condemned [for your hypocrisy]; pardon [others when they truly repent and change], and you will be pardoned [when you truly repent and change]." Luke 6:37 AMP.** The truth is that we can apply the freedom of the forgiveness of the cross to those who have hurt us, and in so doing, we are free from the judgment we have been under because of our judgment towards them.

Forgiveness "does not need to be followed by kind feelings toward the perpetrator...it does not mean that we excuse or ignore sinful actions by another. It means we allow God to deal with the situation or person as He sees fit and to heal our wounds." We never have to excuse or condone the behavior of those who have hurt us. We also do not have to have a relationship with them. It is possible to have forgiveness and freedom as well as boundaries. This is especially true when forgiving those who have been physically and/or sexually abusive. There is no need to call, text, or write the person and tell them you forgive them unless the Holy Spirit instructs you to. Speaking out forgiveness is a powerful weapon against the enemy. You have been given authority through Jesus, and as you speak out words of forgiveness, you become even more free from the bondage of bitterness and unforgiveness. You may also benefit from writing a letter of forgiveness, even if you never send it. It is often cathartic to physically express the pent-up emotions you may feel.

Reese, A. J., & Barnett, J. R. (2008). Freedom Tools (2nd ed., p. 126). Chosen Books.

Releasing Emotions

Earlier, I shared an example of giving God your emotions and allowing Him to heal the wounds on your soul. Releasing emotions is especially important before forgiving. Emotions are important, but they are not our guide. I want to invite you into the process of identifying emotions.

We will begin by praying this aloud: **"Holy Spirit, I ask that you would silence the voice of the enemy and all demonic influence. I ask that you would silence my thoughts and bind my mind to the mind of Christ. I ask that I will only hear from you."** Next, ask Holy Spirit who you need to forgive.

If you, for example, need to forgive your Mom, proceed in praying, "When I think about my mom, I feel..." What emotions pop up? Maybe certain memories come to mind... "When I think about (certain memory), I feel..."

After you have the list of emotions, continue praying, saying, **"Jesus, I give you (emotion). Would you take it from me and would you heal the wound on my soul?"** Continue for every emotion that arises. If you encounter an emotion you sense you have partnered with in negative ways- like anger, resentment, etc- then you can repent and ask Jesus to release you and others from the negative effects.

The Lie: "I Can't Forgive Them."

The gift of the cross is that Jesus died and forgave our sins, and in that He has given us the ability to receive forgiveness and to give it away. As you begin your forgiveness journey, or as you continue on one you have been on, you do not have to create more forgiveness. It is not your job to make up new forgiveness or to wipe the slate clean on your own. You are simply choosing to apply the forgiveness of the cross, bought by Jesus' blood, to those who have hurt you. This takes a lot of the pressure off, doesn't it?

The Lie Breaker

The following prayer is a great one to start you on the journey of forgiveness.

"Father, I come to you now, fully submitted. I desire to lay aside my rights, thoughts, and emotions to allow you to move through me. I confess that I have not always seen this person or organization as you do. I confess that the hurts I have experienced have clouded my eyes. I ask you to allow me to see this person (or organization) like you do. Thank you for forgiving me for so many things. I receive your forgiveness, and I ask you to help me release that same forgiveness to those who have hurt me.

_____(person or organization name) I choose to forgive you for _____ (specifically what they did to you or those you love).

I release you from all of my judgment and remove every debt I have placed on you. I break agreement with vengeance or payback. Lord, remove all bitterness and unforgiveness in me. Father, I repent for anything I have said or done that has grieved you. Please remove all judgment from me and change my heart regarding this person/organization. Jesus, I ask you to reveal yourself to this person/organization and bring them into relationship with You. Father, please take away the spirit of offense and heal every wound on my soul. Holy Spirit, I ask that you nurture me now and help me receive your love. "

Epilogue

It has been an honor to share with you the glory of God's work in my life, and my deepest and most sincere prayer is that it will stir you into greater freedom. I KNOW that the same power that set me free and brought me into marvelous light is working in you, even now. The Lord is mighty to save. He will wait and watch for the time of your surrender and for your choice to allow Him to move in your life. I encourage you to rebuke fear at every turn. **"Submit yourselves, then, to God. Resist the devil, and he will flee from you." James 4:7 NIV.** Fear will attempt to rob you of Christ's confidence and His goodness. As you stand in the authority of Christ, you will watch as circumstances that seemed impossible become possible with the strength and healing of Christ. He will turn some of the hardest nights into days of laughter. He desires that you learn to cast all your cares on Him because He loves you.

You do not have to carry the world's weight, not in your physical body or spirit. He can set you free and help you to walk light. **"Are you tired? Worn out? Burned out on religion? Come to me. Get away with me and you'll recover your life. I'll show you how to take a real rest. Walk with me and work with me—watch how I do it. Learn the unforced rhythms of grace. I won't lay anything heavy or ill-fitting on you. Keep company with me and you'll learn to live freely and lightly."** Matthew 11:28-30 The Message

I pray you learn the unforced rhythms of grace. I pray you will find freedom from the lies you learned about your weight and value and learn what it means to indeed be **Weightless.**
Love,
Jill

Section 2: The Lie Breakers

The Lie: Skinniness is Next to Godliness

The lies that skinniness and your image are as important, or sometimes more than Godliness, is a warped view that the enemy will use to torment you. I want you to grab a piece of paper and a pen. Would you start by praying this aloud: **"Dear Jesus, would you come and reveal to me the lies that I have been believing?"** Now, could you take a moment to let him speak to you? Consider the lies that you have been partnering with and write them down.

The Lie Breaker

Read this prayer aloud with BOLDNESS! Step into the truth God has for you! Pray it daily, if needed. Take every thought captive- literally, grab the negative thoughts Satan spews at you and throw them out. Fill your heart with truth and hope from the Word.

"Father, I repent for agreeing with and I walk away from the lies I have believed that do not line up with your truth. I repent and walk away from self-hatred. I repent and walk away from negative self-talk. I repent and walk away from (Fill in your own here) _____. I receive the forgiveness you bought for me on the cross. I choose to forgive myself for (whatever you still feel angry with yourself about) _____. I receive the truth that I am loved, I am righteous through Jesus, and that my worth is rooted in you. I ask that you would come and heal the wounds on my soul. Amen."

The Lie: It's All My Fault

Receiving the understanding that you are loved and never alone breaks off the lie that it is all your fault. I want you to grab a piece of paper and a pen. Would you start by praying this aloud: **"Father, would you reveal to me the lies that I have been believing about my body, food, and movement?"** Now, could you take a moment to let Him speak to you? Consider the lies that you have been partnering with and write them down.

The Lie Breaker

Read this prayer aloud with BOLDNESS! Step into the truth God has for you! Pray it daily, if needed. Take every thought captive- literally, grab the negative thoughts Satan spews at you and throw them out. Fill your heart with truth and hope from the Word.

"Father, I repent and walk away from the lies I have believed that do not line up with your truth. I repent and walk away from self-hatred. I repent and walk away from self-focus. I repent and walk away from the idol of comfort. I repent and walk away from the idol of food. I repent and walk away from (Fill in your own here) _____. I receive the forgiveness you bought for me on the cross. I choose to forgive myself for (whatever you still feel angry with yourself about) _____. I ask that you would come and heal the wounds on my soul and show me the truths that you want me to know. I receive your love, your light, and your glory. Amen."

The Lie: "I'd Be Valuable If..."

When we seek to find value in sources outside of the inherited, unshakeable value God has given us, we end up wanting. We will continue on and on in whatever way possible, trying to prove to ourselves and others that we are valuable, and we will be led astray, time after time. True value lies on the cross and all that Christ did for us. The Father has adopted us, calling us His own, bringing us into a relationship with Him, and restoring our identity. We must partner with Him in this truth and break agreement with the pervasive lies. Let's do that together...

The Lie Breaker

Pray aloud with me:

"Lord, I repent for agreeing with the lie that I have to maintain my behaviors to be successful and receive my value from those things. I break off all words I have spoken that aligned with that lie and receive the truth that my value is detached from my behavior. I receive the truth that my value is in Christ alone. I receive the truth that my value was established before the earth's foundations, as I am your creation. Lord, I ask that you reveal your love for me and show me how my value is established in you alone. I ask you to build a holy strength in me to be able to do what you have called me to do. I choose to build my life on you alone and not on anything I try to do in my own strength. Thank you for your love and grace. Amen."

The Lie: "I'm Not Worth the Effort..."

A New Start

God has brought conviction as he has shown me how thoughts about my size have ruled me. He has shown me that these thoughts have often taken me captive and kept me in bondage. I have repented of placing my worth outside of truth. Would you like to join me?

The Lie Breaker

Pray aloud with me:

"Jesus, I repent for placing my value in my size, weight goals, and looks in (fill in the blank). I repent for idolizing anything that is not you. I sever any words I have made in partnership with the lie that says I am only worthy if I meet and maintain my goals. I receive the truth that I am fearfully and wonderfully made, complete, and lacking nothing. I receive my worth from your death on the cross and apply your freedom to my body, soul, and spirit. Thank you for loving me unconditionally. Help me to love myself as you do. Amen."

You can repeat this prayer and flow with the Lord in prayer as other thoughts emerge.

The Lie: "Love is All You Need"

The lie that the love of another is enough to fulfill and heal us is so pervasive in our culture. From movies to books and songs, we are taught from a young age that there is love out there waiting for us that will make us whole. The world finds a prince charming, but the Bible teaches us it is King Jesus who comes to save, heal, love, and cherish. He is the one who will fulfill your every need and longing. He is the one who heals every wound. Will you let Him?

The Lie Breaker

Pray aloud with me:

"Holy Spirit, thank you for revealing these areas where I have allowed deception to rule in my heart and mind. I repent for allowing other loves to fill your position in my heart. I reject and walk away from any lies I have believed or spoken over myself and ask that you remove their effects on me. I ask that you fill me with your Spirit and flood me with truth where lies have dwelled. Would you fill my body, soul, and spirit with your love? I ask, Father, that you show me how you love me and fill me with the ability to receive that love. I choose to receive the freedom of the cross and love myself as you love me."

The Lie: "I am Not Enough."

From the perspective of the world, we will never be enough. Our culture and industry require that we will want to continue buying all the new clothes, new makeup, new supplements, new skincare, etc. Every ad seeks to reach those who have a 'need.' This doesn't mean you shouldn't buy new items; just start recognizing that in Christ, you are enough. Is your beauty and significance firmly planted in that truth? If not, why? What lies have you believed that have kept you from that truth?

The Lie Breaker

Pray aloud with me:

"In the name of Jesus Christ, I sever the lie that I am not enough. Through Jesus Christ, I am made holy, acceptable, and sufficient by His will and strength. I repent for agreeing with the lie that I can and should be perfect. I repent for trying to control my life. I release myself from my judgment. I receive the truth that I am the righteousness of God in Christ Jesus and that by His blood I have been redeemed and walk in His authority. I receive my identity from God alone. I receive my value from the cross. Thank you, Jesus, for dying for me, living in me, and bringing me into true freedom. Amen."

The Lie: "God is Not Enough."

God is incredibly faithful, and He is not angry with you if you have stepped into believing that He is not enough. He desires that you repent for idolatry, turn away from faulty thinking, and be restored to the truth that He is good and true, and can always repair any broken place in your life. He loves you deeply.

The Lie Breaker

I invite you to pray aloud:

"Holy Spirit, I invite you to reveal all the ways I have believed you are not enough. Please show me what I have allowed to become idols in my life. I repent for making _____ (state your idols) an idol and for allowing it/them to become more important than you. I repent for not trusting you with my whole heart. I ask that you would tear down and remove everything that has been exalted above you and that in their place, you would sit, enthroned in my heart. I choose to trust you. I choose to relinquish control and repent for trying to control my own life. I need you, I love you, and I give you permission to have your way. Would you come, Holy Spirit, and fill me, and change everything?"

The Lie: "I'll Never be Free."

God is incredibly faithful, and He is not angry with you if you have stepped into believing that He is not enough. He desires that you repent for idolatry, turn away from faulty thinking, and be restored to the truth that He is good and true, and can always repair any broken place in your life. He loves you deeply.

The Lie Breaker

I invite you to pray aloud:

"Dear Jesus, Thank you for choosing me, as the joy set before you when you went to the cross. Thank you for dying for me and for making way for me to live free from all bondage and sin. I repent for taking things into my own hands. I repent for trying to live my life under my terms. I repent for not allowing you total access and control. I confess and repent for committing the sins of _____ (list your sins and those known in your family line, i.e. adultery in the family.) I receive your forgiveness over myself and my family line. I thank you, Jesus, for coming and bringing healing into my body, soul, and spirit. Thank you for healing every wound on my soul. Would you bring me into a deeper knowledge of you and your love for me? I give you all of me. I love you. Amen."

The Lie: "I Can't Forgive Them."

The gift of the cross is that Jesus died and forgave our sins, and in that He has given us the ability to receive forgiveness and to give it away. As you begin your forgiveness journey, or as you continue on one you have been on, you do not have to create more forgiveness. It is not your job to make up new forgiveness or to wipe the slate clean on your own. You are simply choosing to apply the forgiveness of the cross, bought by Jesus' blood, to those who have hurt you. This takes a lot of the pressure off, doesn't it?

The Lie Breaker

The following prayer is a great one to start you on the journey of forgiveness.

"Father, I come to you now, fully submitted. I desire to lay aside my rights, thoughts, and emotions to allow you to move through me. I confess that I have not always seen this person or organization as you do. I confess that the hurts I have experienced have clouded my eyes. I ask you to allow me to see this person (or organization) like you do. Thank you for forgiving me for so many things. I receive your forgiveness, and I ask you to help me release that same forgiveness to those who have hurt me.

_____(person or organization name) I choose to forgive you for _____ (specifically what they did to you or those you love).

I release you from all of my judgment and remove every debt I have placed on you. I break agreement with vengeance or payback. Lord, remove all bitterness and unforgiveness in me. Father, I repent for anything I have said or done that has grieved you. Please remove all judgment from me and change my heart regarding this person/organization. Jesus, I ask you to reveal yourself to this person/organization and bring them into relationship with You. Father, please take away the spirit of offense and heal every wound on my soul. Holy Spirit, I ask that you nurture me now and help me receive your love. "

Author's Note

This book has been a labor of love with you at the heart of it all. It has been a joy to write how God has healed my heart and set me free, hoping that he will do the same for you through these pages and throughout the rest of your life. I pray that reading this book has led you into the depths of truth God has written over your life. His Word is full of promises regarding you. Jesus is always ready and waiting to walk with you through life's joys and pains. He is praying for you, and so am I!

As I was writing toward the end of this book, I realized that I was actually writing a second book, a workbook. The Lord kept placing questions on my heart to provoke the reader to action. I realized these questions needed space, so I created the Weightless Workbook.

The Weightless Workbook will help you actively pursue wholeness in your body, soul, and spirit by walking through a deeper dive into each chapter with questions that lead to action and repentance and into the understanding of total freedom through deliverance. I pray that you will grow and prosper as you journey through the Workbook. You can join the private Facebook Group **Weightless Warriors** to work through the Book and Workbook together and to find community as you go.

Please join the group and share your stories and testimonies as the Lord leads; I cannot wait to hear what God does in your life.

All my love and prayers,
Jill

Section 3: Notes & References

eternal	*eternal*	*temporary*
# Spirit	# Soul	# Body
Gifts of the spirit	Mind	Systems
Supernatural senses	Desire	Health
Faith	Will	Senses
	Reason	Organs
	Personality	Physical shell
	Emotion	
	Fruit of the Spirit	
	Thought	

Resources

Aside from the Bible, the following ministries, books, and podcasts are some resources that have greatly benefited me in my journey. As I share, I encourage you to seek the Lord in what and who you allow to speak into your life. He is your teacher, and He will guide you.

The Core Group	coregroupmentorship.com
North Georgia Tres Dias	ngtd.org
Pastor Dan Mohler	neckministries.com
Holy Spirit Encounter	holyspiritencounter.org
The God Chasers	by Tommy Tenney
100 Days of Believing Bigger	by Marshawn Evans Daniels
Healing the Orphan Spirit	by Leif Hetland
The Finger of God	by Torace Solomon
Spiritual Authority	by Watchman Nee
There is More Podcast	With the Perry's Podcast
Remnant Radio Podcast	Green Room Podcast

Scripture Index

Lie #1: "Skinniness is Next to Godliness."
Ecclesiastes 3:11 AMP (p. 6)
Matthew 11: 28-30 The Message (p. 7)
1 Peter 5:8 AMP (p. 7)
James 4:7 AMP (p. 7)
John 10:10 AMP (p. 11)
Ephesians 6:12 AMP (p. 11)
Ephesians 6:10-11 AMP (p. 11)
2 Corinthians 10:5 The Message (p. 12)
Ephesians 6:13-17 AMP (p. 12)

Lie #2: "It's All My Fault"
Romans 8:1 AMP (p. 15)
1 Corinthians 6:19-20 TPT (p. 16)
Isaiah 61:3 NKJV (p. 25)
Acts 17:28 AMP (p. 27)

Lie #3: "I'd be Valuable If"
1 Corinthians 9:25-27 TPT (p. 38)
Philippians 4:13 AMP (p. 42)

Lie #4: "I'm Not Worth the effort."
Ephesians 1:5-6 TPT (p. 46)
Romans 8:15-16 ESV (p. 47)
Prov 23:7 AMP (p. 49)
James 3:5-6, 8 TPT (p. 49)
Proverbs 18:8 AMP (p. 49)
Philippians 4:8 AMP (p. 53)
2 Peter 1:3 TPT (p. 53)
James 1:17 TPT (p. 53)
Romans 5:8 TPT (p. 53)

Lie #5: "Love is All You Need"
Genesis 2:24 AMP (p. 61)
Proverbs 18:21 AMP (p. 61)
Mark 12:31 TPT (p. 62)
Galatians 5:24 TPT (p. 63)
Romans 5:8 TPT (p. 63)
2 Corinthians 11:14 AMP (p. 64)
Jeremiah 17:9 AMP (p. 64)
Romans 5:8 TPT (p. 66)
Phillippians 2:3-4 AMP (p. 66)
Ephesians 1:17-18 AMP (p. 68)
John 17:21-23 TPT (pp. 69-70)
John 15:7 AMP
Romans 8:34 NIV (p. 71)
Zephaniah 3:17 NIV (p. 72)
Psalm 139:13-14 AMP (p. 72)
Ephesians 2:10 AMP (p. 72)
1 Peter 2:9 AMP (p. 72)
Zephaniah 3:17 AMP (p. 72)

Lie #6: "I'm Not Enough."
John 15:5 TPT (p. 75)
2 Corinthians 12:9 TPT (p. 76)
Colossians 1:13-14 NIV (p. 78)
John 8:36 AMP (p. 78)
Psalm 37:4 AMP (p. 78)
Hebrews 13:5 AMP (p. 78)
Isaiah 54:10 AMP (p. 79)
Ephesians 2:8-9 TPT (p. 79)
Psalm 139:16-18 TPT (p. 83)
Ephesians 1:11 TPT (p. 84)
1 Peter 1:4 TPT (p. 84)
Ephesians 1:3 TPT (p. 84)

Lie #7: "God is Not Enough."
Luke 12:34 AMP (p. 89)
1 Kings 11:4 NIV (p. 90)
Exodus 32:1 NASB (p. 90)
1 John 5:18-21 (p. 99)

Lie #8: "I'll Never Be Free."
Thessalonians 5:23-24 TPT (p. 102)
Psalm 51:5 NIV (p. 104)
Proverbs 20:27 AMP (p. 104)
Romans 6:6-7 AMP (p. 104)
Matthew 10:8 AMP (p. 105)
John 14:12-14 AMP (p. 105)
2 Corinthians 6:14 AMP (p. 107)
1 Kings 22:6-7 AMP (p. 107)
1 Kings 22:19-23 (p. 108)
Mark 5:6-13 AMP (p. 109)
Luke 21:19 NKJV (p. 109)

Lie #9: "I Can't Forgive Them."
Ephesians 4:30-32 TPT (p. 112)
James 4:6 NIV (p. 113)
Hebrews 12:14-17 NIV (p. 114)
Matt 6:14-15 TPT (p. 116)
Luke 23:24 AMP (p. 117)
Matthew 26:28 TPT (p. 117)
Luke 6:37 AMP (p. 118)
Matthew 18:21-22 TPT (p. 121)

Epilogue
James 4:7 NIV (p. 122)
Matthew 11:28-30 The Message (p. 123)

About the Author

Jill Blue is a Holy Spirit-led counselor and mental health coach with a heart to guide others into the freedom she's experienced in her own life. Having personally walked through miraculous healing from cancer and deliverance from lies and inner turmoil, Jill knows firsthand the power of God's restorative love. These experiences have fueled Jill's passion to see others find wholeness in Christ, and today, she dedicates her life to helping women and individuals uncover the truth of their identity and purpose in God. Jill's compassionate and spirit-driven approach is marked by gentle but firm guidance, encouraging each person she works with to listen to the Holy Spirit, trust God's promises, and discover the transformative love of Jesus. She believes that healing is not just possible but available to all of God's children, and she is honored to walk alongside others as they experience this life-changing freedom.

Furthermore, Jill believes we are mind, body, AND spirit- and that all three play an important role in an individual's healing and breakthrough. Jill's story of resilience and unwavering faith serves as a powerful testament to God's unshakeable power, inspiring others to confront challenges with courage, authority, and surrender. She believes that every individual carries a divine purpose and is passionate about helping God's children step into the fullness of their identity in Christ, free from shame, fear, and past pain. To learn more about booking Jill for speaking engagements and to work with Jill in a coaching capacity, visit **www.coachjillblue.com**.

Jill lives in Canton, Georgia, with her husband, Desmond. They passionately love the Lord and enjoy serving on their church's worship team, as well as Vida Nueva and Tres Dias of North Georgia, two ministries close to their hearts. They provide pre-marital and marital coaching and love seeing marriages heal and thrive. If you want more information on pre-marital or marital coaching, visit **www.coachjillblue.com**.